Ireland

FOR BEGINNERS

Phil Evans &
Eileen Pollock

Writers and Readers

My share of this book is for my friend John Walker.
Phil

Henry John and Rosie are for Christine, with love from
Polly

Writers and Readers Publishing Cooperative Society Ltd.
144 Camden High Street, London NW1 0NE,
England

First Published by Writers and Readers Publishing
Cooperative Society Ltd. 1983

Series Editor Richard Appignanesi
Cover design by Louise Fili

Printed in Great Britain at
The University Press, Oxford

Cased: ISBN 0 86316 016 6
Paper: ISBN 0 86316 017 4

Contents

NOW READ ON...

HENRY JOHN

IN THE BEGINNING was the word and the word was Conquest. So, when they'd been overrun by the Gaels (Guidel), the Cruithne of Little Britain (Ireland), known as Scots (Irish), the original Hibernians (Ivernii) conquered the Pictish Kingdom of Dalriada (of the Uluti) in Ulster (Ulidia), and Scotland (Alba), taking with them the language of the Gaels (Scotti).

Needless to say by the time St Patrick was sold in slavery to a Cruithnic chief of Ulster (Ulaid) the real Irish (of Scotia major) were the Lowland Scots (of Scotia minor). Naturally enough, Ulster (Uladh), therefore became the cradle of Christianity which brought Europe out of the Dark Ages, for all the thanks we ever got.

Eventually of course the Scots came back like homing birds bringing progress and democracy with them. They saved Ireland for the Crown, got persecuted for their pains, and emigrated in their thousands to become the flower and backbone of American Society. Oh yes. Once there, of course, they established Religion, put down the Indians, won the West and by their democratic example inspired the Presbyterians of the North to rise against Dublin Corruption, the result of which was the Union which we have been defending ever since, for which persistent loyalty we are once again persecuted.

Only this time we're going nowhere.

History of Ireland, there you have it.

Henry John lives off Sandy Row
His parlour house is damp and cold
Toilet's in the yard, you take a torch,
   it frightens off the rats
And though the kitchen ceiling leaks
That house is kept meticulous
That way it looks more Protestant
Says Henry John.

ROSIE

ARE YOU sitting down?

Because I'm going to shock you now — There was History in Ireland long before the first Englishman ever set foot in the place!

There was indeed. There were clans and tribes and warring kinglets, all happy as larry out fighting and making a name for themselves. There was eight kinds of marriage, eight kinds of divorce, and a woman or a husband or a slave could still fetch a reasonable price in cattle. What there wasn't was 100% total adherence to the letter of the law of the Christian principles laid down by St Patrick.

And all the Saints and all the Scholars and all the illuminated manuscripts campaigning to keep the clergy celibate and the language rid of dirty words was to no avail.

St Patrick sent down a message to the Pope.

"Listen, mate," he said (for the Pope was an Englishman). "Something has to be done."

"Nay," said the Pope. "Eying naw frafflayah heppayah barta stewshun! Pripps irongate Herritoo Bullyittin samsorshay. Hes joy god."

And do you know, credit where credit is due, he was as good as his word!

Rosie lives just off the Falls
Two up, two down and an outside bog
Kids get sent to granny's while their
*   Daddy has his weekly bath*
There's no hot water in the tap
But every day the step gets scrubbed
For cleanliness is godliness
So Rosie says.

The Pope

In terms of misery you wouldn't think there's much to choose
But Henry John maintains he has a lot to lose
In the land of the blind the one-eyed man is King.

In May 1169, the Normans land at Bannow near Waterford.

They come from Wales, at the express invitation of the defeated Irish king of Leinster, **Dermot MacMurrough**. Dermot enlists their aid to recover his kingdom, in return for promises of

Only a thousand men, in this first invasion, prove more than a match for the Irish forces. The Normans are mounted, wear sophisticated mail, and are backed by disciplined bodies of archers. They are also veterans — battle hardened Norman mercenaries who have conquered Britain and half of Europe.

They terrify the townsfolk of Wexford, who surrender after a short siege.

Dermot is

'ONE WHO PREFERS TO BE FEARED RATHER THAN LOVED, WHO IS OBNOXIOUS TO HIS OWN PEOPLE AND AN OF HATRED TO STRANGERS. HIS HAND IS AGAINST EVERY MAN, AND EVERY MAN'S HAND AGAINST HIM.'

DERMOT.

WATERFORD

WEXFORD

Pour ne pas se présenter à visage découvert, la bourgeoisie a introduit dans le champ social une instance formellement séparée d'elle comme de la classe dominée, jouissant d'une autonomie relative, mais qui lui permet en définitive, et globalement, d'assurer et de reproduire son exploitation économique et de perpétuer sa domination politique.

Dermot, with his Norman ally, **Strongbow**, advances to Dublin and sacks it. On the way Dermot indulges in an orgy of killing. Irish politics has always been a grisly business.

Walking among the severed heads of 200 men after a battle in Kilkenny, Dermot spots '...the head of one he mortally hated. Taking it by the ears and hair he tore the nostrils and lips with his teeth.'

(Dermot will die in 1171, as a writer at the time records with satisfaction, 'of an intolerable and uncommon disease. He became putrid while living, by the miracles of God...')

Henry II of England is initially delighted to see the Normans of Wales busy elsewhere. Many of them hold illegitimate claims to titles and land in England, and are persistent troublemakers. Later, he begins to fear that they may set up a rival state.

Henry extracts from the Pope a Papal Privilege known as the 'Laudabiliter'. This grants 'the hereditary possession of Ireland' to Henry. The Pope is **Adrian IV**, originally Nicholas Breakspeare, the only Englishman ever made Pope.

9

With 4,000 men-at-arms and 500 knights, Henry lands at Waterford in 1171. No need for battle. Henry is a brilliant diplomat. He brings the Normans to heel, tours the country, and offers the remaining Irish kings their land back in return for 'protection'.

Henry is formally installed as Lord of Ireland, but the invaders hold only a small enclave in Dublin, harassed by Irish from the hills, woods, and bogs.

Dublin is repeopled by Henry, mainly with Bristolians. It is declared a 'no-go' area for the Irish. This area of 30 square miles, surrounded by a palisade, becomes known as the Pale. Irish found inside are hunted down and killed.

By 1367 the conquerors of Ireland, wearied by the subversive influence of Irish culture upon their Anglo-Norman 'Way Of Life', pass the Statute of Kilkenny.

It:

• Bans intermarriage with the Irish
• Bans the adoption of Irish names, dress, customs or speech.
• Fines anyone 'harbouring or encouraging Irish minstrels, rhymers, or taletellers'.
• Forbids those holding land granted by the Crown to allow the Irish to graze cattle.

Nobody takes any notice. The puppet Parliament of the Pale lacks the resources to enforce the decrees. Besides, many powerful Anglo-Normans have 'gone Irish'.

10   * Kiss my arse!

The English Protestant Reformation, carried through by **Henry VIII**, changes all this. In 1541 he has himself declared 'King of this land of Ireland as united, annexed and knit forever to the Imperial Crown of the Realm of England'.

Crown and nobility alike expel peasants from the land to make room for profitable sheepwalks, creating a vast army of vagrants.

You can't put these sheep on our land – what's going to happen to **US**?

You'll go the same way as Anne Boleyn and Catherine Howard if you don't shut up!

You tell 'em, Henry!

Henry's successor, the Catholic **Mary**, 'plants' English settlers on newly emptied 'shire-land'.

The great Irish lords resist the attack on their independence. They appeal to the Pope. Small Catholic expeditions in 1579 and 1580 land at Dingle and Kinsale.

Reprisal

The English response is ferocious. The poet **Edmund Spenser** describes the scene:

'ERE ONE YEAR AND A HALF THEY (THE REBELS) WERE BROUGHT TO SUCH WRETCHEDNESS AS THAT ANY STONY HEART WOULD HAVE RUED THE SAME. OUT OF EVERY CORNER OF THE WOODS AND GLENS THEY CAME CREEPING FORTH UPON THEIR HANDS, FOR THEIR LEGS WOULD NOT BEAR THEM; THEY LOOKED LIKE ANATOMIES OF DEATH; THEY SPOKE LIKE GHOSTS CRYING OUT OF THEIR GRAVES; THEY DID EAT THE DEAD CARRIONS, HAPPY WHERE THEY COULD FIND THEM... THE VERY CARCASSES THEY SPARED NOT TO SCRAPE OUT OF THEIR GRAVES; AND IF THEY FOUND A PLOT OF WATER CRESSES OR SHAMROCKS, THERE THEY FLOCKED AS TO A FEAST FOR A TIME... IN SHORT SPACE THERE WERE NONE ALMOST LEFT, AND A MOST POPULOUS AND PLENTIFUL COUNTRY SUDDENLY LEFT VOID OF MAN OR BEAST.'

In 1601 the last resisting nobleman, **O'Neill**, Earl of Tyrone, is decisively defeated at Kinsale. He flees abroad in 1607 in the famous 'Flight of the Earls'.

> Don't weep. They'll be back when the multinationals move in!

> This night sees Eire desolate,
> Her chiefs are cast out of their state;
> Her men, her maidens weep to see
> Her desolate that should peopled be.
>
> Man after man, day after day
> Her noblest princes pass away
> And leave to all the rabble rest
> A land dispeopled of her best.

SIR PHILLOM O'NEILL

Plantation

The best known of all Plantations, that of Ulster, is carried out in 1609. Scottish and English 'Undertakers' are given the largest plots, and forbidden to have Irish tenants. Loyal 'Servitors' of the English government in Ireland are allotted smaller portions. The 'Natives' — the Irish — are sold barely one-tenth of the available land, at exorbitant prices.

UNDERTAKER

Charles 1

In 1640 the simmering conflict between **Charles I** of England and his Parliament boils over. Charles represents the bankrupt landowning nobles, living on taxation. Parliament stands for the interests of the growing capitalist class.

In October of 1641 the Irish clans rise. They sweep the planted areas of Ulster clear of colonists, who take refuge in the towns. There are rumours in England that rebels have 'massacred every Protestant in Ireland'. In fact, 3,000 Protestants are killed; perhaps 7,000 more die of exposure.

Parliament, naturally, will not trust Charles with an army to crush the rebels, who fight under the slogan 'Pro Deo, Pro Rege, Pro Hibernia Unanimis' ('One for God, King and Ireland'.)

These years are a period of confusion in Ireland, with Charles intriguing to raise an Irish Army. They end with Charles' execution in Whitehall, 'a man of blood, false to his word, and an enemy of the people of England.'

Cromwell

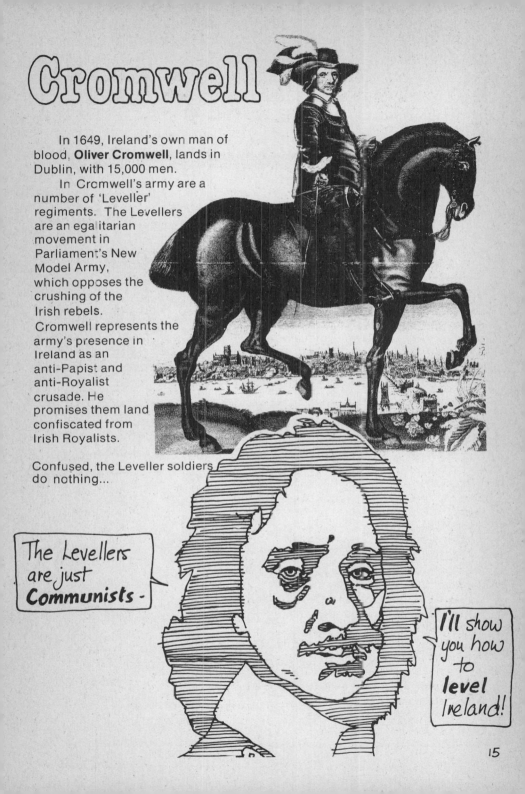

In 1649, Ireland's own man of blood, **Oliver Cromwell**, lands in Dublin, with 15,000 men.

In Cromwell's army are a number of 'Leveller' regiments. The Levellers are an egalitarian movement in Parliament's New Model Army, which opposes the crushing of the Irish rebels. Cromwell represents the army's presence in Ireland as an anti-Papist and anti-Royalist crusade. He promises them land confiscated from Irish Royalists.

Confused, the Leveller soldiers do nothing...

The Levellers are just **Communists** -

I'll show you how to **level** Ireland!

To this day in rural Ireland the oath 'The curse of Cromwell on you' can be heard. With good reason. His army sets out on a campaign of unequalled savagery. In his own account of the attack on the first rebel town, Drogheda, the garrison does not surrender.

'Being thus entered, we refused

Drogheda

DROGHEDA

them quarter; having, the day before, summoned the town.

'I believe we put to the sword the whole number of the defendants. I do not think Thirty of the number escaped with their lives. The enemy were about 3,000 strong in the town.

It hath pleased God to bless our endeavours at Drogheda...'

All 'friars' and priests are 'knocked on the head as soon as seen'.

The same pattern is repeated at Wexford, Waterford and Limerick. Remaining garrisons surrender when 'summoned'.

Eye-witnesses describe conditions:

'Whole counties had been depopulated.

'A man might travel twenty miles and not see a living creature, either man or beast or bird.

'As for the poor commons, the sun never shined upon a nation so completely miserable.'

'YOU ASK WHAT I HAVE FOUND, AND FAR AND WIDE I GO:

NOTHING BUT CROMWELL'S HOUSE AND CROMWELL'S MURDEROUS CREW,

THE LOVERS AND THE DANCERS ARE BEATEN INTO THE CLAY,

AND THE TALL MEN AND THE SWORDSMEN AND THE HORSEMEN, WHERE ARE THEY?'

W. B. Yeats

Parliament imposes a 'Settlement'. It drives Catholic landlords from their land, into barren Connacht. Small tenants are forced to follow. Cromwell's soldiers are rewarded with 'tickets' for land.

Protestants now hold more than 75% of cultivable land. One quarter of the Catholic population is dead; thousands more are deported to fever-ridden colonies or sold to the West Indies as slaves.

I know - let's all sing 'When Irish Eyes Are Smiling'!

In 1660 the English monarchy is restored. But **Charles II** needs the support of Parliament: Catholic hopes are dashed as the Restoration Act of Settlement confirms Cromwell's measures — only to rise again on the succession of **James II** as King of England and Ireland in 1685. For James is a Catholic. The Catholic-dominated Irish Parliament repeals the Settlement.

The Pwotestant weligion is wong!

James II

I always look this miserable because I know I'm going to be held responsible for all the bad things that are going to happen!

William.

'OUR GOOD KING JAMES IS A BRAVE AND HONEST MAN, BUT THE SILLIEST I HAVE EVER SEEN IN MY LIFE'
French Courtier.

Catholic hopes are short-lived. The English Parliament decides to overthrow James. They send for his son-in-law, **William of Orange** of the Netherlands, a fervent Protestant.

The deposed James decides to raise an army in Ireland.

Landing at Kinsale in 1689 he lays siege to the city of Derry ('Londonderry' to Protestants). The Protestants in the city, led by the Apprentice Boys, hold out.

The Apprentice Boys march in triumph to this day, under the slogan 'No Surrender'.

NO SURRENDER

Aren't they a bit old to be apprentices, Mam?

They're slow learners, child!

Battle of the Boyne

William of Orange.

Up the Shankill* boys!

On July 1st 1690 James and William's armies meet at the Boyne. William's army is a hotch-potch of Scots, Ulstermen, Dutch, Danes, Swedes, Prussians and French Huguenots. (Parliament refuses him men: 'He has plenty of Dutchmen anyway.')

The armies are fairly evenly matched; but James makes disastrous tactical errors. William's troops cross the river and chase James' troops back to Dublin.

James bravely leads the retreat.

Retiring officers in James' army shout to the enemy:

Crowning victory for the 'English' army comes at the battle of Aughrim, where in a ferocious engagement 7,000 of an Irish-Franco army are slain. James is nowhere to be seen.

HENRY JOHN

"HERE'S TO our Sovereign Lord, King William of Orange and his descendants, who saved us from Pope and Popery, brass money and wooden shoes, and he who will not drink this toast may he be quartered, damned and doubly jammed into the roaring cannons of the North. To Hell with the Pope, up King Billy and a fart to the Bishop of Cork!"

No doubt about it, the Pope of Rome is behind every misfortune this country has ever seen. The Pope? Don't talk to me about the Pope, the Pope doesn't know which side's up. Wasn't he intervening on the side of Charles against Parliament one day and backing King Billy of glorious and immortal memory the next? Allegiances and alliances and God knows what all — Fickle as a Woolworth's weathervane and about as infallible as his own much vaunted rhythm method! A stranger to democracy from generation unto generation, that's your Pope.

Democracy... is what the majority wants. The minority has just got to wait its turn to get into a majority. Our trouble here has always been that our minority can't be *let* get into a majority or they'd destroy us all. Nothing complicated about that.

People say there has been discrimination here against Roman Catholics. There has been *no* discrimination here against Roman Catholics. What there has been is an attempt to prevent subversives infiltrating key sectors of the community: civil service, heavy industry, public services, security forces — disloyal elements whose aim is the destruction of Ulster.

Of course in England they make us out to be halfwits when we talk of loyalty. But they won't let the Heir Apparent marry one, will they? Oh drop a *class* or two, no problem. But any talk of marrying a Fenian and you're talking treason.

ROSIE

I WOKE UP one morning, I thought I was in the Wild West. The Army had moved in overnight and consolidated themselves here there and everywhere in fortified stockades. We call ours Fort Knox.

Then, as if this wasn't excitement enough for one day, they treated us to a spate of ransackings the same afternoon. If it was only vampires you could string garlic round the house, but there's no stopping them boys. That was the time they lifted our Michael and did him for burying guns in the back garden.

Well, I didn't know whether to take a mother's pride in the wee lad's ingenuity or what, for we haven't got a back garden.

I went down to the court when his case came up, they wouldn't let me in. This big policeman stopped me at the door. I says, "Excuse me, I am the boy's mother. I demand my rights." Do you know what he said? This here is the God's honest truth. "Missus," he said, "You have no rights." That there is what he said.

And I know that peeler too. Owen Rogers is his name. He's a Fenian and all so he is. See, they do have a certain quota of Roman Catholics on the police force.

"I do a job," says he. "Full stop. No ifs, or buts, or whys or wherefores. This is a democracy, I represent the law. If you have a quarrel with the democracy it is my job to protect you are treading on dangerous ground, Rose McCusker and you'll go the way of your wee skitter of a son". "Well, Owen Rogers," I says, "You've come a long way. But I don't see why you bother to do the job so well, because they're not going to promote you, not till some Catholic sergeant retires, dies of disillusionment or gets shot."

I got escorted home by four Welsh soldiers and an Alsatian dog.

Between 1695 and 1705 the Irish Parliament passes a series of Penal Laws. Under these Acts:
- Catholics are barred from public office.
- They are barred from the army and navy.
- They cannot vote.
- A reward of £5 is offered for the head of a priest.(The same as that on the head of a wolf.)

The Penal Laws change land ownership. No Catholic can buy land, or lease it for more than 31 years. The laws of inheritance are changed so that any Catholic's child who converts to Protestantism becomes the heir.

A proposal to castrate captured priests is never enacted ... Catholic gentlemen having a gun are liable to whipping — and will have any horse confiscated if it is 'worth more than £5 ...'

The mass of the Irish peasantry live in destitution and virtual serfdom, under a Protestant 'Ascendancy' backed by the Penal Laws and the gallows.

All gentleness and hospitality,
All courtesy and merriment is gone;
Our virtues withered every one,
Our music vanished and our skill to sing:
Now may we quiet us and quit our moan,
Nothing is whole that could be broke; nothing
Remains to us of all that was our own.
JAMES STEPHENS.

'Hedge-schools', run by travelling schoolmasters keep alive some tradition of literacy and Gaelic culture.

Illicit Catholic worship survives, using round flat-topped rocks as altars hidden in the woods. (Many of these, pointed out today, are as likely to be leprechauns' pool-tables as altars.)

OK—who carved 'KILROY WAS HERE' on the stone altar?

KILROY WAZ HERE

Jonathan Swift, author of 'Gulliver's Travels' writes: 'By unmeasurable screwing and racking their rents all over the kingdom, (the landlords) have already reduced the poor people to a worse condition than the peasants in France, or the vassals in Germany or Poland'.

Swift recommends that –

...the carcass of a good fat child... will make four dishes of nutritious meat... I grant this food will be somewhat dear and therefore **very proper for landlords** who, as they have already devoured most of their Parents, seem to have the best title to the children.

GULLIVERS TRAVELS

— Jonathan Swift.

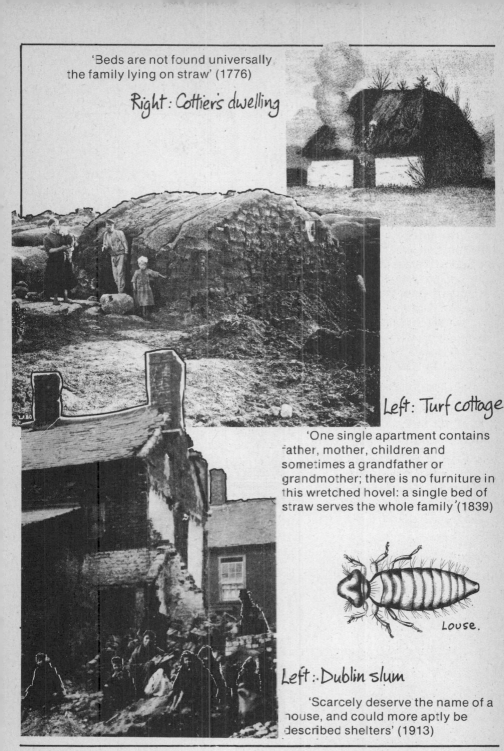

'Beds are not found universally the family lying on straw' (1776)

Right: Cottier's dwelling

Left: Turf cottage

'One single apartment contains father, mother, children and sometimes a grandfather or grandmother; there is no furniture in this wretched hovel: a single bed of straw serves the whole family'(1839)

Louse.

Left: Dublin slum

'Scarcely deserve the name of a house, and could more aptly be described shelters' (1913)

By 1711 a number of secret societies develop in the countryside. By night, wearing white shirts, with blackened faces, they carry out reprisals against rackrenting landlords.

Fifty years later the 'Whiteboys' movement rides about the countryside at night tearing down new fences enclosing land, beating up rent collectors and intimidating landowners. Other groups call themselves 'Moonlighters', 'Oakboys'; 'Steelboys'; 'Peep O'Day Boys'. The last two are organisations of poor Protestants operating at 'peep o' day'.

'Ribboners' wear a white ribbon round the head to distinguish them in the dark.

These societies dispense rough and ready justice, but have few political ideas.

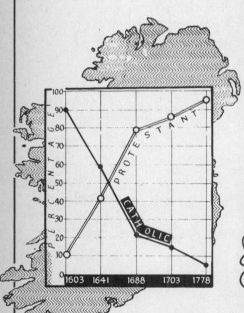

Above: percentage change in land ownership 1603–1778

Two revolutions have a deep effect on popular Irish politics. The American Revolution of 1776 and the French Revolution of 1789.

In Ulster, Protestants organise an army of Volunteers, to defend Ireland against the 'peril' posed by the American colonists.

The Government is powerless to stop the growth of the Volunteers. When it makes feeble attempts to do so, it drives Protestants and Catholics together.

The Volunteers pass a Declaration of Irish Right which:

French revolutionary plate

• Declares the Irish Parliament to be the only body which can make laws for Ireland (though recognising the King as 'King of Ireland'
• Declares 'As men, as Irishmen, as Christians, and as *Protestants*, we rejoice in the relaxation in the Penal laws against our Roman fellow-subjects ...'

Well! I never thought I'd be marching side by side with a —

—Protestant!

—Catholic!

VOLUNTEERS

Protestant or Catholic—they're all Paddies!

Henry John's father.

HENRY JOHN

YOU SHOULD HEAR my father! Round here they call him Papish Tom. There's no harm in him like, he's just a bit, you know, soft in the head, simple. Well his favourite story is about the unemployment riots in the 30's...

"I mind the time," he goes... even the wee uns know it word for word... "I mind the time I came home from work and I says to your Mammy, that's it, we're going on strike, there's not a fella on Outdoor Relief going to do one tap of work the morra'. Until they up them rates, there'll be no more work done, they can do their worst," he says... And begod, you know, they very nearly did.

Apparently there was barricades up the Shankill, barricades up the Falls, oh aye, Fenians and all was at it, shouting, hurling bricks at the peelers, all the starving hordes of Belfast were out. Well, there's a bit of a lull up the Shankill, and the lads are just standing about waiting and this big red faced woman comes up and she says that the peelers are laying into the Fenians on the Falls, and she yells: "Are youse going to let them down, are yez?" — The Fenians, like! — And they all roar back, "No, by Jeez, we are not!" And away they all charge in their hundreds, screaming and shouting, and my father in the lead with his wee wheelbarrow full of half bricks. He spoke to one of them that day. Gerry Lynch was his name. "Gerry," he says, "We are all in the same boat, and that there boat is sinking fast. Never again will they divide us, Gerry," he says. "Never again."

NEVER AGAIN....

Well then, fortunately, they discovered it for the Fenian plot it was and that was the end of that. But my father, ach, he must have got a crack on the head with a peeler's truncheon that day. Damaged his brain.

ROSIE

OUR MAJELLA usually does the cleaning for me on a Saturday while I'm out doing the shopping. Well, here dear, last Saturday I come in through the back door and the first thing I notice is the tap on the sink — gleaming like a ray of sunlight in the middle of our wee pokey kitchen. I called Majella in and asked her was she feeling alright. She's not a dirty child, but this was unprecedented to say the least.

Apparently she was giving it the usual splish, splosh, splish, quick lick and out to play, when suddenly she remembers what Sister Mary Thomasina had said in school about the problems of Communism. It appears that Communists always make a point of doing everything better than anybody else, you see, and that's why they're so dangerous.

Majella was mortified. She had betrayed the Baby Jesus! He had died for her on the Cross and she couldn't even do the taps for Him right down to the gundgy bits. And if she couldn't even do the taps for Him right down to the gundgy bits, how could she be expected to ward off the advancing Marxist hordes who were even now forging their way westwards across Europe, eyes firmly fixed on God's own Jewel of Ireland?

I haven't been so angry since she donated all my spare blankets to the African Missionary Fund, on the understanding that if they got enough spare blankets from Holy Ireland, the assorted African peoples would cast off their sinful pro-communist ways and devote themselves to a life of spiritually uplifting squalor.

"If you put the same energy into helping me pester the Authorities for a decent house, daughter," I said, "We'd maybe have a kitchen that was that much easier to clean."

the French Revolution

You lot won't know what to do without me to tell you!

The American Revolution produced the Volunteers. The French Revolution now throws up the Society of United Irishmen. Its leader is **Theobald Wolfe Tone.**

'Our independence must be had at all hazards. If the men of property will not support us, they must fall: we can support ourselves by the aid of that numerous and respectable class of the community — *the men of no property.'*

The class Tone looks to which can bring about this change is not always the 'men of no property'. He struggles — like **Robespierre** in France, or **Paine** in England — to bring about conditions in which the rising capitalist class (the bourgeoisie) can develop unhindered by the rotting hand of feudal monarchy.

Wolfe Tone.

Theobald Wolfe Tone was born in Dublin on June 20, 1763. His family is 'low' Protestant (as opposed to Anglican). He is 16 when the French Revolution shakes Europe. On the second anniversary of Bastille Day Tone proposed at a celebration that:

- English influence in Ireland is the great grievance of the country.
- That the most effective way to oppose it is by a reform in (the Irish) Parliament.
- That no reform can be 'just or efficacious' which does not include the Catholics.

His third proposition is greeted with hostility in his Protestant circles. Tone at once writes 'An Argument on Behalf of the Catholics of Ireland by a Northern Whig'. He argues that reform can only come about by Protestant-Catholic unity against their 'one common enemy', and that the 'depression and slavery of Ireland is produced and perpetuated by the divisions existing between them'. This strikes a chord in radical circles in Belfast and Dublin.

He is invited to help in the formation of a 'Society of United Irishmen' in Belfast. With the help of his friend **Thomas Russell,** an army officer, and **Napper Tandy,** he forms a Dublin Society.

The 'Koran' of the movement, as Tone puts it, is Thomas Paine's *Rights of Man,* which is published in 1792.

The Society seeks:

- Manhood suffrage.
- Equal electoral districts (Ireland is riddled with 'rotten boroughs').
- No property qualification for voters.
- Annual parliaments.
- Payment of MPs.

Tone writes in his diary, on the execution of Louis XVI: 'The King of France was beheaded. I am sorry it was necessary.'

He notes that it is becoming fashionable for Dubliners to address each other as 'citizen', like the French.

The Guillotine.

The Society welcomes **Mary Wollstonecraft's** *Vindication of the Rights of Woman*

Left: Mary Wollstonecraft
Below: George Bernard Shaw.

In February 1793 war breaks out between England and France. The British Government clamps down on radical and militant peasant movements in Ireland. The active Irish secret society of the Defenders, an armed organisation which raids the houses of the great landlords, is fiercely repressed. Hundreds are hanged, as belonging to a 'secret Junto, that like the French Jacobins, wish to throw all government into confusion'. And: 'but being yet alive, should be cut down, but being alive their bowels be taken out and burned before their faces.'

You're a Catholic Michael — what are you doing in the militia?

It's good pay — thirty pieces of silver!

The Government keeps a careful eye on the Society's activities, using a widespread network of informers. At the same time it passes the Catholic Relief Act.

This Act is not intended for the relief of Catholics. It raises bans on Catholics becoming soldiers, but enables the raising of a native Catholic militia, under Dublin Castle's control, to counter insurrection in the Irish countryside.

In France, Tone sets out to convince the generals that a French invasion of Ireland will be greeted by an uprising. He has a frustrating time.

'I am utterly ignorant whether there is any design to attempt the expedition or not.'

At last, on 16 December, 1796, 43 French ships, carrying 14,000 troops, set sail for Ireland from Brest, with Tone aboard. The expedition is dogged by misfortune. One of the ships imediately strikes a rock and sinks, drowning 550 of its crew. The flagship gets lost, with the admiral on board. Storm, followed by thick fog and a head wind at last sees the arrival of most of the fleet in Bantry Bay. Another gale blows up, preventing a landing, although Tone records bitterly:

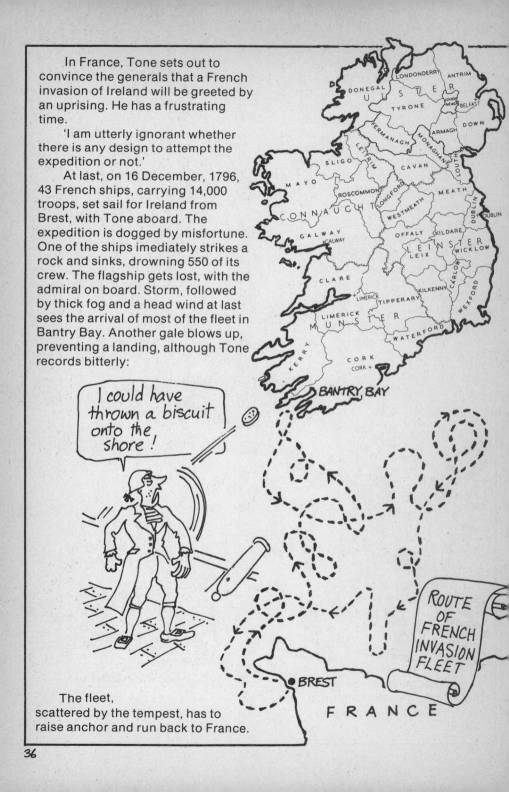

The fleet, scattered by the tempest, has to raise anchor and run back to France.

Dublin Castle, panicked by the appearance of the French, starts a reign of terror against the United Irishmen and all Catholics. Martial law is enforced with militia from England. An Orange Yeomanry is encouraged to establish 'law and order'. This turns into an orgy of murder, looting and rape. To extract confessions about hidden arms they resort to:

'Picketing — a variety of crucifixion in which the victim is fastened, back to the ground, his wrists and ankles drawn to full stretch by cords tied to picket pegs; half-hanging; pitch-capping (crowning the victim with a linen cap filled with boiling pitch); roasting the soles of the victim's feet at a turf fire...'

The population resists. They gather crops for those in prison, and openly 'wish the French would come'.

The French *do* come again; three times.

Tone and the United Irishmen are now faced with a choice: revolutionary France is at war with reactionary England. Tone spells out his strategy:

'England's difficulty is Ireland's opportunity.'

So you see, Napper,

'In a word, from reason, reflection, interest, prejudice, the spirit of change, the misery of the great bulk of the nation, and above all the hatred of the English name, resulting from the tyranny of near seven centuries —

— there seems little doubt that an invasion in sufficient force would be supported by the people. There is scarcely an army in the country, and the militia, the bulk of whom are Catholics, would to a moral certainty refuse to act —

THWAP!

— if they saw such a force as they could look to for support.'

Are you listening, Napper?

*∴öoz//

In 1795, as the Government seizes and tries members of the Society, Wolfe leaves for America. He is bound for France.

In 1795 too, a small battle takes place near Armagh on a piece of ground called the Diamond. A party of Catholic 'Defenders' attack a group of Protestant 'Peep o' Day Boys' — and are beaten, leaving thirty dead.

The Battle of the Diamond passes into popular Protestant mythology. The Peep o' Day Boys celebrate by renaming themselves the Orange Society:

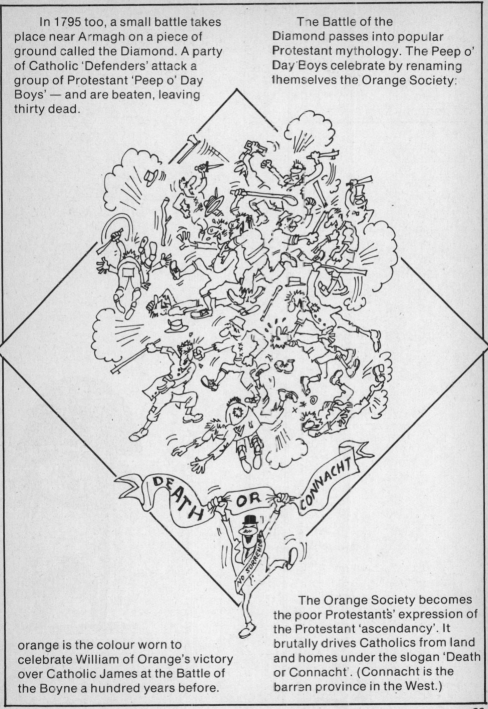

orange is the colour worn to celebrate William of Orange's victory over Catholic James at the Battle of the Boyne a hundred years before.

The Orange Society becomes the poor Protestants' expression of the Protestant 'ascendancy'. It brutally drives Catholics from land and homes under the slogan 'Death or Connacht'. (Connacht is the barren province in the West.)

On the morning of October 12, 1798, a British squadron intercepts and defeats the last French expedition of ten ships with 3,000 men. Wolfe Tone comands a French battery and scorns escape in a fast French schooner. The French surrender after a 4-hour battle against the more heavily armed British. Tone is taken to Dublin in irons for trial.

Brits bearing 0200!

Success is all in this life... I have failed to emancipate my country... I have done my duty and I have no doubt the Court will do theirs. I have only to add that a man who has thought and acted as I have done should be armed against fear of death.

Tone is sentenced to hang.

On the morning on which he is to be executed Tone is found lying in his cell with his throat cut. Friends — and his son — maintain he has been attacked by his gaolers. The gaolers say he cut his own throat. After a week of agony he dies, none but the prison doctor being allowed near. There is no inquest.

Tone leaves two ideas behind him: Ireland should be separated from the Crown it shares with England: only unity between Protestants and Catholics can bring about this Irish republic.

In 1800, the English Parliament, panicked by the rising, passes the Act of Union. Ireland henceforth is to be part of Britain. It will send 100 MPs to Westminster as part of a 'United Kingdom'.

the Act of Union

In August 1798, the French commander, **Humbert**, with a thousand men, disembarks at Killala. he expects 'a numerous and well-disciplined army' will rise in support; but finds a disorganised, badly armed, fearful peasantry. Some Irish do join, and Humbert's force fights bravely. But, isolated and weak, they are soon forced to surrender. The French are treated fairly well (Humbert is returned to France), but the hundreds who rose in support are treated barbarously.

A smaller French force, with Napper Tandy aboard, lands in mid-September on Rutland Island, off Donegal. It issues a fine proclamation:

Merde! Où est l'armé Irlandaise très professionelle? Voici seulement trois paysans mal armés avec des batons sportifs!

United Irishmen... strike on their blood-cemented thrones the murderers of your friends... wage a war of extermination against your oppressors, the war of liberty against tyranny!

HIC!

There is no response. The population cannot read English. Napper Tandy gets drunk and is carried back on board. They sail away. (Tandy later dies in France.)

> The Soldier smiling hears the Widow's Cries,
> And stabs the Son before the Mother's Eyes.
> With like Remorse his Brother of the Trade,
> The Butcher, feels the Lamb beneath his blade.
>
> Jonathan Swift: On Dreams

In the County of Wexford the population sleep in the fields at night, fearful of capture and torture by the yeomanry — who are mainly Catholic — and British militia.

In May, 1798, a body of cavalry encounters a group of peasants armed with pikes. The cavalry captain is killed. Burnings and reprisals force the peasantry of Wexford into rebellion.

The Battle of Vinegar Hill.

At the battle of Vinegar Hill, where they raise the green flag in a last stand, the peasants are broken by artillery fire. 'They fell like mown grass'. The king's troops show no mercy to the defeated. '...hundreds and thousands were butchered while on their knees begging for mercy; and it is difficult to say whether soldiers, yeomen or militia men took most delight in their bloody work.'

The officer who observes this adds that 25,000 rebels and peaceable inhabitants have been killed. Historians say 50,000 died.

43

Robert Emmet hatches a new conspiracy in 1803. It is shrouded in a veil of misty romanticism. It has the right ingredients for a myth: the young idealist — the failed rising — the love for a woman leading to capture — hanging — martyrdom.

Robert Emmet.

In fact it is a bungled parody of the theory and practice of the United Irishmen. Emmet's ideas are based on the *coup*. A small elite band is to seize Dublin Castle and then call on the masses, who will rise — taking advantage of the authorities' confusion. Emmet forgets that the masses will be just as surprised as the government.

Emmet's elaborate system of signals to his various supporters collapses; the coup develops into a street brawl.

Emmet has not the sense to leave his middle-class girlfriend and flee. He is captured and hanged.

A sad sidelight is that Wolfe Tone's brave and loyal friend, Thomas Russell, becomes embroiled in the abortive coup. He is also sent to the gallows.

No Act of Union can wipe out the fact that Ireland's relation to England is as an economic appendage.

The country is plagued with middlemen. Grossly inflated land rents force peasants abroad for part of the year to make up their arrears from wage labour. These are hungry years in England too, but in England workers are exploited as a class. In Ireland they are also exploited as a subject nation.

'That is why, when agitation in England took the form of working-men's Chartism, in Ireland it took the form of a National agitation for a repeal of the Union...'

Below: An English worker presents the 'Charter' demanding democratic reforms. 1839.

Under the leadership of **Daniel O'Connell** the agitation for repeal shakes Ireland. O'Connell has already been the leading spirit in the campaign for Catholic Emancipation, passed in 1829, which allows Catholics to become MPs and hold commissions in the army. It makes O'Connell's reputation as a Westminster MP and as an orator and tactician.

"A GENTLEMAN IN DIFFICULTIES;" or, DAN AND HIS "FORCES."

'Punch' 1846

The campaign for repeal is more difficult. O'Connell is backed by the radical 'Young Ireland' group, and the *Nation* newspaper. The *Nation* particularly exasperates O'Connell by pushing for more and more radical demands, forcing the old man to 'keep up'.

It is O'Connell's idea to hold a series of 'Monster' meetings to demonstrate popular feeling for Repeal. They are indeed huge. A meeting at Mallow is half-a-million strong.

People covered the plain as far as the eye could see.'

As many turned up to meetings at Mullaghmast and Tara. Some observers put the numbers at Tara — the old seat of the great king of Ireland — at a million. Considering that the population of Ireland at this time is about 8 millon this is a staggering turnout. *Protestants join the movement in a great national consensus.*

The 'Monster' meetings seriously alarm English businessmen, fearful that mass agitation may spread to English workers demanding the 10-hour day. The Government moves troops to Ireland.

O'Connell plans a final 'Monster' meeting at Clontarf, bigger than all the others, with support from England. At last the Government moves.

The day before the planned rally, Saturday October 4th 1843, Dublin Castle bans the rally. It is a tense moment.

For O'Connell, constitutional by instinct, the decision is easy. The giant he has created threatens to take on a life of its own, out of his control.

He calls it off.

Thousands — hundreds of thousands — already on the way are turned back, including massive contingents from England already in Ireland. The Government breathes a sigh of relief. So does O'Connell. A survivor of the 1798 Rising remarks caustically:

This Monster Rally – should we send in the troops?

No – we'll send in O'Connell !

Ireland was won at Clontarf*, and at Clontarf it was lost again !

Daniel O'Connell

* King Brian Boru defeated the Danes at Clontarf in 1014.

REPEAL

48

the Great Hunger

In 1845 a disaster strikes Ireland which makes land reform and Repeal lock insignificant. It is the first year of the Great Starvation. In the autumn of 1845 a potato blight reaches Ireland from America. In 1846 it worsens with a wet spring. By the end of the year people have eaten their seed potatoes for the next year. A magistrate of Cork, **Nicholas Cummons**, reports on a visit to the village of Skibbereen:

'I entered some of the hovels... and the scenes which presented themselves were such as no tongue or pen can convey any idea of. In the first, six famished and ghastly skeletons, to all appearances dead, were huddled in a corner on some filthy straw, their sole covering which seemed a ragged horsecloth, their wretched legs hanging about, naked above the knees. I approached with horror, and found by a low moaning they were alive — they were in fever, four children, a woman and what had once been a man. It is impossible to go through the detail. Suffice it to say, that in a few minutes I was surrounded by at least 200 such phantoms, frightful spectres as no words can describe, either from famine or fever... My heart sickens at the recital...'

Searching for potatoes in the Famine.

A Famine funeral.

Ireland is not the only country to suffer a failure of the potato crop. But it is the only country to suffer such disastrous famine. Why? Because of Ireland's relationship with England. During the famine years the country produced bumper crops of oats; wheat, barley and vegetables. These are not used to feed the people. **Fintan Lalor**, the great Irish land reformer, explains:

EAT–

DRINK–

The potato perished; the landlord took the crop. The tenant-cultivator paid his rents – was forced to pay them – sold his grain crop to pay them, and had to pray to man as well as God for his daily bread.

Fintan Lalor

But man and God didn't help us.

–AND BE MERRY!

During the years of the Starvation, 1845-51, more than a million people die of hunger and subsequent diseases, like typhus and cholera.

Emigration

And the famine sets off another disaster: mass emigration. Faced with starvation, people head for the ports. In January 1847, the Poor Law Guardians, in one week alone, dispense relief to 130,000 people. In the ten years after 1845 two million Irish people — *a quarter of the population* — leave Ireland for ever.

Population in Ireland (millions)

1811	5.9
1841	8.2
1851	6.5
1976	4.7

Goodbye Mum — I'll be back as soon as I've earned enough to send over the fares for Eithne and Mary and Eamonn and Patrick and Molly and Fiona and Michael and Bernadette and Seamus and Oona...

Mum — your dinners in the oven
xxx
Margaret.
P.S. I've gone to Australia

Waiting on the quay...

They go to the United States, Canada, Britain, and a smaller number to Australia and New Zealand. Often the passage is undertaken in fearful conditions. In 1847 the *Virginus* sails from Liverpool to Quebec with 476 Irish emigrants. 158 passengers die and 106 catch fever, including the captain.

Evictions following inability to pay rent are the major cause of the new catastrophe. Landlords are eager to clear land for more profitable grazing land. **Marx** writes:

1,032,694 Irish people were replaced by 996,877 head of cattle!

the Evictions

Six crowbar men, from distant
     county brought —
Orange, and glorying in their work
     'tis thought,
But wrongly — churls of Catholics
     are they
And merely hired at half-a-crown
     a day.

THE NATION 1d.

LALOR LASHES EVICTIONS

URGES ALLIANCE WITH CHARTISTS

Priest struck by lightning

O'CONNELL DIES

Delorean offers cash guarantee

PIG FARMING IN TYRONE

In three hours more
You find, where Ballytulagh stood before,
Mere shattered walls, and doors
     with useless latch,
And firesides buried under fallen thatch.

Lalor, a frail man; almost a hunchback, is a strong supporter of the *Nation*, and *Young Ireland*. He differs from O'Connell in putting land reform at the centre in the fight for national independence. Marx and his collaborator **Engels** concur:

❝ The most urgent need is to end the forcible eviction of peasants and to stop the landlords, backed by the English authorities, from robbing the Irish farmers of their livelihood.' This must be the main object for the Irish national liberation movement' ❞

Lalor was not a reformist.

'The landlords have adopted the policy of depopulating the island, and are pressing it forward to their own destruction, or to ours. They are declaring that they and we can no longer live together in this land. They are enforcing self-defence on us. They are, at least, forcing on us the question of submission or resistance: and I, for one, shall give my vote for resistance.'

He's a terrible troublemaker, that Lalor!

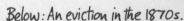

Below: An eviction in the 1870s.

The British Government rushes a Sedition Act through Parliament.

SEDITION ACT

IRELAND

A PRESENT FROM ENGLAND

Are you arming Brother Protestants,
Are you arming for the fray,
Are you resolved on victory,
And crushing Papal sway?

Quantities of arms are sent to reliable Orange lodges by Dublin Castle.

The Irish conspirators are seized on charges of 'treason-felony' before the instructions for a general rising can be transmitted. An abortive insurrection at Ballingarry, in Tipperary, fizzles out. The leadership of the movement receives long terms of transportation.

AUSTRALIA

BOTANY BAY

In the general election of 1852 a Tenant Right League campaigns on the '3 F's' — Free sale, Fixity of tenure, and Fair rent — and wins 40 Irish seats out of a total of 103.

The Tenant Right League falls into the hands of parliamentary careerists. It is nicknamed '<u>The Pope's Brass Band</u>', and collapses after an embezzlement scandal.

In 1858 a new movement is born, simultaneously in New York and Dublin. The Irish Republican Brotherhood is better known as the 'Fenians', named after the followers — the 'Fianna' — of the legendary **Finn MacCumhal**. The Fenians are revolutionaries.

the Fenians

I am an Ulsterman, a Connachtman, a Greek.
I am Cuchulain, I am Patrick.
I am Carbery-Cathead, I am Goll.
I am my own father and my son.
I am every hero from the crack of time.

Finn MacCumhal.

— AND IM A FENIAN!

56

During the American Civil War of 1861 thousands of Irishmen fight — on both sides. (The famous 3D photographs of the war are taken by an Irish-American, **Matthew Brady**.) The Fenians see it as a chance to learn to use arms. By the end of the War 200,000 Irish soldiers have been sworn in as Fenians.

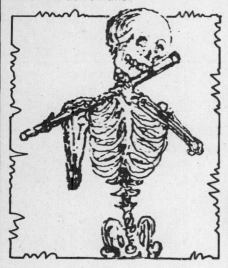

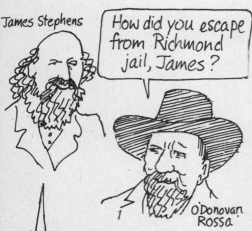

James Stephens

How did you escape from Richmond jail, James?

O'Donovan Rossa

Easy, O'Donovan — two of the warders were Fenians!

In 1863 they found the *Irish People* — the Fenian paper. Its editors are close friends of Fintan Lalor. The journal is vital in building the Fenian's underground organisation. In 1865 the British move against the Fenians.

Their most influential leaders are arrested, including **James Stephens**, member of Karl Marx's International Working Men's Association — and **Rossa** (real name **O'Donovan**), a fiery Fenian organiser. The swoop beheads the organisation. Stephens makes a famous escape from Richmond Prison, Dublin, but the organisation is crippled.

In 1867 the Fenians attempt an insurrection. But the authorities are forewarned by their network of informers. Messages to Fenian strongholds in Kerry and other areas are bungled, causing confusion about the date of the rising, and a fierce blizzard sets in.
Communications also fail during a bold attempt to seize the arsenal at Chester Castle.

The dispirited rebels drift home through the snow — to face mass arrests and deportations.

Two further incidents in Britain mark the decline of Fenianism, the Manchester Rescue and the Clerkenwell explosion. In the first, armed Fenians release Republican prisoners from a prison van — but accidentally shoot a **Sergeant Brett** dead. Three of the rescue party are captured and hanged, although none of them fired the fatal shot. A wave of revulsion sweeps Ireland at the execution of the 'Manchester Martyrs'.

Frederick Engels writes:

All the Fenians lacked were martyrs. These they have been presented with...

At Clerkenwell prison Fenian sympathisers explode a keg of gunpowder outside the gaol walls in an attempt to free a Fenian organiser. The explosion backfires, and demolishes a row of tenements, killing 7 and injuring 120. There is a backlash of public outrage against Irish revolutionaries.

THE FENIAN GUY FAWKES.

Fenians in America plan to attack Canada in 1866. 'We promise', declares the general in charge of the raid, 'that before the summer sun kisses the hill-tops of Ireland, a ray of hope will gladden every true Irish heart. The green flag will be flying independently to freedom's breeze, and we will have a base of operations from which we can not only emancipate Ireland, but also annihilate England'. 800 armed Fenians cross the river Niagara. Two days later at Ridgeway they fight a battle with a group of Canadian student volunteers — losing 8 dead. (The Canadians lose 12.) Then, short of supplies, and leaving sixty captured Fenians, they are forced to return across the border.

Fenian headquarters announces:

Beaver

As a military conspiracy the Fenian movement fails, but it demonstrates to the British a determined Irish nationalism. **William Gladstone** confesses that it is the Fenian rising in Ireland which awakened him to

The vast importance of the Irish question...

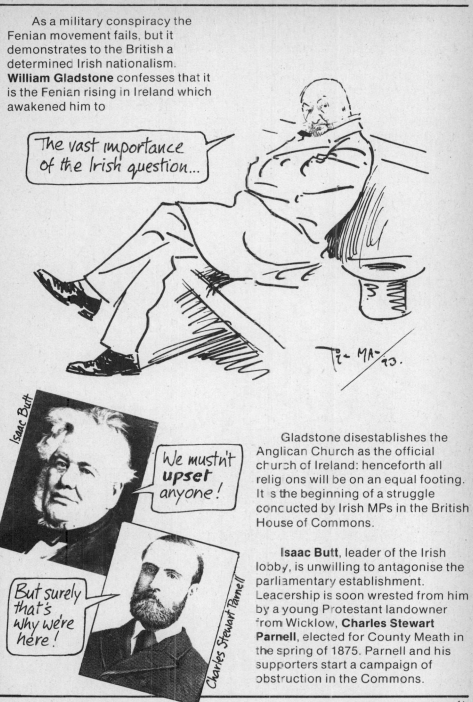

We mustn't **upset** anyone!

But surely that's why we're here!

Isaac Butt

Charles Stewart Parnell

Gladstone disestablishes the Anglican Church as the official church of Ireland: henceforth all religions will be on an equal footing. It is the beginning of a struggle conducted by Irish MPs in the British House of Commons.

Isaac Butt, leader of the Irish lobby, is unwilling to antagonise the parliamentary establishment. Leadership is soon wrested from him by a young Protestant landowner from Wicklow, **Charles Stewart Parnell**, elected for County Meath in the spring of 1875. Parnell and his supporters start a campaign of obstruction in the Commons.

On of the Home Rulers is **Joseph Biggar**, a wholesale port merchant — and a secret member of the Supreme Council of the Irish Republican Brotherhood. When the Prince of Wales attempts to take a seat in the gallery of the Commons to hear a debate on horse-breeding Biggar shouts out 'I spy strangers!' Under the rules of the House, the Speaker is forced to clear the gallery. Biggar is condemned as 'ungentlemanly'.

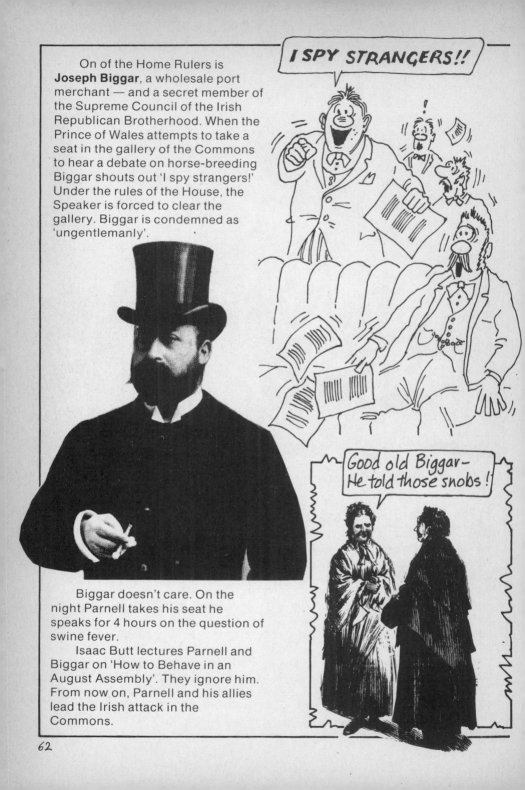

I SPY STRANGERS!!

Good old Biggar— He told those snobs!

Biggar doesn't care. On the night Parnell takes his seat he speaks for 4 hours on the question of swine fever.

Isaac Butt lectures Parnell and Biggar on 'How to Behave in an August Assembly'. They ignore him. From now on, Parnell and his allies lead the Irish attack in the Commons.

A fresh economic crisis threatens Ireland. Falling prices, crop failures and wet weather cause mass bankruptcies, starvation, and a fresh wave of eviction of small farmers who cannot pay the rent.

Evicted families storm a government workhouse. But it is full...

the Land League

Michael Davitt founds the Irish National Land League. Davitt is a brilliant organiser and theoretician. As a child of 11 he lost an arm minding a machine in a cotton mill. In 1870 he is sentenced to 15 years' penal servitude for Fenian agitation, of which he serves 7, in Dartmoor. He founds the *New Departure* on his release, an alliance of parliamentary and revolutionary forces, on the issues of the land question and self-determination for Ireland.

HENRY JOHN

THERE'S A LOT of people desperate to die for Ireland. I have to laugh. The whiskey is produced by Americans, the Waterford glass by Belgians, the mines are all Canadian... it's open season for the steam-roller-borders-so-we-can-get-at-you-better brigade.

The daughter Sadie got a wee job with one of these international concerns that had bought up a department store here. They put her on the picture counter. Not that she's the slightest bit artistic, she's like me, she couldn't draw breath.

So then, one day, the Big Chief Managing Director from England arrives for to see why they're not pulling in his 37½% profit he claims he has to have. Do you know, every day they all got issued with sales performance sheets for the same day the previous year, the whole sales staff, and if they didn't continually top them figures by the required amount they were in serious bother. That's a fact.

So there's our Sadie all dolled up for his supreme Managership and he comes round and he points to this picture and he says: "What about that one there?" And our Sadie says, "Sure you couldn't give that one away, sir!" laughing, like and gushing all over him. "My dear young lady," he says, "I'll have you know *I* was the sales representative who *sold* that picture to this shop five years ago, and if *I* could sell it to you, you can sell it to somebody else!"

She was raging! Half a bottle of perfume she'd wasted!

Two months later they pulled out. Couldn't get their 37½%. Merchant Adventurers wouldn't be in it. Only these ones don't give a sod about ye. No matter how loyal and Orange you are. And still the government is running to them, waiting on them hand and foot — subsidies, free factories! But I'll tell you something for nothing now, they are digging their own graves, Quite frankly, assuring jobs for disloyal elements while staunch supporters of the state are going around jobless, is tantamount to digging their own graves.

all gushing...

ROSIE

MY SISTER BERNIE went down south to the Republic to live. Mad Irish. Always was. Fluent speaker too and all that. I don't know where she got it from for we couldn't rub two words of Irish together in our house. But anyway, away she went. Off to Dublin in the green. Hanging out the window of the Dublin express, glowing with patriotic fervour, singin' "Thank God we're surrounded by Water!"

"Here," I says to her, "You needn't be thinking you'l be necessarily better off down there in the South. Because apart from ending up further down the housing list than we are..." (Oh, and have you heard the latest? They're not building any more houses up the road. "It's a Green Belt" said the man. I said the only belt you need round Belfast is black belt in Karate)... "Apart from that," I says, 'They're a hair's breadth away from hanging people down there."

"Ach," she says, "That there's not the point, at least you're with your own." D'you see our Bernie — I'll say this much for her, she's very good with her hands, and she has a beautiful singing voice, but she is stupid. "What Own?" I says. For personally it gives me no satisfaction knowing that the fella cutting my throat was educated by the same nuns as me. You find the exact same mentality down there among the so-called leading lights — haven't the guts to do the exploiting themselves, so they're selling out, *giving* out all round them to these multinational outfits. Considering they have only such second rate ambitions for themselves, I doubt if they can have anything very lofty in mind for the likes of our Bernie!

A beautiful singing voice.

Parnell speaks at a land-meeting in 1879 at Westport:

'Hold a firm grip of your homesteads and lands. You must not allow yourselves to be dispossessed as your fathers were dispossessed in 1847.' Parnell becomes President of the Land League.

The League fights against evictions and for rent reductions in the 'Land War' of 1879-82. It leads to the creation of a new word, 'boycott'. Parnell explains:

Boycott

When a man takes a farm from which another has been evicted, you must show him on the road-side when you meet him, you must show him in the streets of the town, you must show him at the shop counter, you must show him in the fair and the market-place, and even in the place of worship, by leaving him severely alone — putting him in to a kind of moral coventry — isolating him from his kind like the leper of old — you must show him your detestation of the crime he has committed.

Three days later **Captain Boycott** finds himself on the receiving end of this policy. Boycott is an estate agent for a **Lord Erne** who refuses the rent offered by his tenants and orders evictions. All farmhands and servants at the Boycott property disappear. Shopkeepers will not serve his household. Police have to deliver his letters. No-one will speak to the Boycotts.

The Captain complains to the London *Times*. The upper classes are horrified: workers everywhere laugh at the Captain who has to do his own washing.

Fifty Orangemen from Ulster volunteer to harvest the Captain's crops. They march through deserted villages, past shuttered shops. It is useless; everything has to be done under massive police protection. In despair, Captain Boycott resigns his position and retires to England.

Enraged at the success of the 'boycott', the state charges the League's leaders and Parnell with 'seditious conspiracy'. Parnell cites — and produces — the evicted inmates of Castlebar workhouse in County Mayo as witnesses for the defence. A conviction cannot be obtained.

NOT GUILTY!

-Until we bring in a new Bill!

In desperation the Government introduces a 'Coercion Bill'.

Parnell and his supporters in the Commons attempt to filibuster the Bill to death by repeatedly moving that the Bill's sponsors 'be no longer heard'. One-by-one the Parnellites are suspended from the House. But they are back the next day.

When the Bill is finally passed, the Government is forced to introduce the Land Act of 1881, which goes a long way towards the Land League's demand for the traditional 'Three Fs'.

- Fair rent.
- Fixity of tenure.
- Freedom for the tenant to sell his interest in his holdings.

When the Land League is paralysed by arrests and repression Parnell's indefatigable sister Anna keeps the movement alive through the 'Ladies' Land League'.

Do you want to join the Land League, Sir?

In 1882, Gladstone makes a deal with Parnell and the large numbers of those arrested for Land League agitation. **Lord Frederick Cavendish** and his under-secretary **Burke** are sent to Ireland to conciliate. On the day of their arrival, in Dublin's Phoenix Park, the anarchist terror group, the 'Invincibles' savagely stab them to death.

THE HUMAN SACRIFICE
Stanley lay extended on the altar . . . a withered hand like a claw was laid on his forehead . . .

The Irish people are a really shocking abominable people - not like any other nation!

Queen Victoria.

The British take the opportunity to introduce a new, even harsher, Coercion Act. Five ex-Fenians are charged with the murder. One of them, **James Carey**, turns informer and is pardoned. The others are hanged. Carey takes a ship for South Africa, but is shot dead on board by another ex-Fenian, **Patrick O'Donnell** — who is himself hanged.

In 1889 the London *Times* is humiliated in a scurrilous attempt to blacken Parnell's name by linking him with the Phoenix Park murders. The 'letters' it produces as evidence are proved to be blatant forgeries.

But disaster strikes Parnell in 1890. Divorce court proceedings reveal that for ten years he has been having a passionate affair with **Kitty O'Shea**, the wife of a former member of the Home Rule Party, one **Captain O'Shea.**

Gladstone, who has presented the fight for Home Rule as a 'moral crusade' demands Parnell's retirement, temporarily at least, from leadership of the Liberal/Irish bloc in the Commons. Parnell refuses — and splits the campaign for Home Rule when Gladstone issues a 'He goes, or I do' ultimatum. Parnell fights three by-elections on the issue of the independence of his Irish party from the Liberals. He loses all three. The Catholic Church and his enemies play on the O'Shea scandal to discredit him politically.

My God — Parnell wants freedom **and** sex!

Gladstone

Exhausted and demoralised — but still campaigning — Parnell dies in Brighton in the arms of Kitty (now his legal wife) in October 1891.

the Gaelic League

Ireland not free only, but Gaelic as well: not Gaelic only, but free as well

Padraig Pearse

In 1892 the Gaelic League is founded, in the footsteps of the so-called Anglo-Irish literary revival. The latter is led by **William Butler Yeats** and includes talents like **George Russell, J.M. Synge, George Moore**, and **James Stephens**. The League grows around the slogan 'A country without a language is a country without a soul' *(Tír gan teangain, tír gan anam)*.

It is an attempt to refresh Irish politics through a revival of Irish culture.

Ní 'IRISH LITERATURE' a bhfuil scríobhtha ag James Joyce adeir-sé, acht tá an teidal sin ion-luaidhte aige i dtaobh 'SEADHNA' leis an Athair Ó Laoghaire. Ní bhainfidh an té a leigh an dá leabhar tatneamh as an ráiteas sin. Gan bacadh leis an focal 'IRISH', is litríocht den chéad aicme 'ULYSSES' agus ní litríocht ar chor ar bith, olc nó maith, aon líne a scríobh an t-Athair Peadar. Is féidir leat (má tá an léigheann agat rud nach bhfuil) 'ULYSSES' a léigheamh i Seapanais acht ní féidir 'SEADHNA' a léigheamh fiú i mBearla.

Myles na Gopaleen
(The 'Irish Times')

Irish chieftain in full dress

William
Butler
Yeats

Yeats writes in
Cathleen Ni Houlihan:

'It is a hard service they take that help me. Many that are red-cheeked now will be pale cheeked; many that have been free to walk the hills and the bogs and the rushes will be sent to walk hard streets in far countries; many a good plan will be broken; many that have gathered money will not stay to spend it; many a child will be born and there will be no father at its christening to give it a name. They that have red cheeks will have pale cheeks for my sake; and for all that they will think that they are well paid.

*'They shall be remembered for ever,
They shall be alive for ever,
They shall be speaking for ever,
The people shall hear them for ever.'*

MICHAEL McCARTAN WAS MURDER BY R.U.C. CONSTABLE McKEOWN. HE WAS SHOT IN THE BACK WHILE PAINTING SL

Yeats has much bitter experience to draw from.

In terms of population alone, 1841's 8 million-plus is reduced to 4½ million by the first decade of the 20th century by famine and emigration. (Today it is still under 5 million.) Then, growth of cities causes new problems of slums, unemployment and health. Dublin in particular has appalling housing conditions at the turn of the century, with exceptionally high child mortality.

Increased contact with the outside world causes a sharp decline in the numbers speaking Irish only: from 64,167 in 1881, to 16,873 in 1911. The Gaelic League sets out to halt the erosion of Irish culture, and what it sees as a demoralising loss of identity. By 1903 it has 600 branches.

With the regeneration of literature comes a revival of Irish sports like hurley and Irish football; folk songs and stories; dancing and historical study. Padraig Pearse, in the Gaelic League at 16, becomes fluent in Gaelic and supports it with pamphlets and stories, plays, essays and poems in Irish.

Pearse enthuses:

'Thanks to the Gaelic League... Irishmen are beginning to realise that they possess a language of their own, which, for antiquity, may vie with the languages of Homer and Virgil, and, for youthful vigour and literary capabilities, with the languages of Dante, Shakespeare, and Goethe.'

Orangeism

'The word of God makes all plain; puts to eternal shame the practices of persecutors, and stigmatises with enduring reprobation the arrogant pretences of Popes and the outrageous dogmata of their blood-stained religion.'
(Thomas Drew, Protestant preacher. Sermon 1867)

'If guns were made for shooting
Then skulls were made to crack
You've never seen a better Taig*
Than with a bullet in his back.'
Songbook published by John McKeague, 1970)

Catholic

What happened to Mc Keague?

Somebody shot him!

I don't mind them killing each other— as long as it doesn't affect business!

After the United Irishmen's rebellion of 1798 — led by the Protestant Wolfe Tone — is crushed, the allegiance of Protestants in the North of Ireland is divided. Militant anti-Catholic Orangeism is strong among the big landlords and small tenant farmers. The businessmen of Belfast, however, incline to liberalism — it's better for expanding industry and free trade abroad.

Following the union with Britain in 1800 Belfast starts to share the benefits of the growth of the British Empire. In 1801 20,000 live in Belfast; by 1901 the population is 350,000. The city has thriving linen, engineering and shipbuilding industries. The new prosperity draws the Protestants of the North away politically and socially from the rest of Ireland, which has mainly tiny struggling industries crushed by British competition.

The city has a sizeable Catholic minority. There are Protestant riots in 1835, 1843, 1864, 1872, 1880, 1884, 1886 and 1898 — usually taking the form of pogroms against Catholics following the annual Orange celebration of the Battle of the Boyne.

———

In 1872 the rioting goes on for days. Much blood is shed in the 'Battle of the Brickfields'. Starting as an attack by fifty armed men from the Protestant Shankhill Road against the Catholic Falls Road, it turns into an orgy of looting, sectarian violence and killing.

All who lost their lives in the Brickfields were Catholics

The *Northern Whig* describes the mobs:

'With guns and pistols, and blades like
crystals.
And stick and bludgeon, and stone
and sling,
And the police eyin' the brickbats flyin'
And the kilties* dancin' the Highland
Fling.

* **Highland Infantry**

75

the Orange card

Home Rule agitation in the 1870s and 1880s alarms the Ulster Protestants. They don't want to share the backwardness of the rest of Ireland, though the living standards of the poor Protestants are grim enough.

Randolph Churchill, a Tory (and father of **Winston**), writes to his friend **James Fitzgibbon**, Chief Justice for Ireland:

I decided some time ago that if Gladstone went for Home Rule, the Orange card was the one to play.

RANDOLPH CHURCHILL PLAYS THE ORANGE CARD.

As early as 1866 **Harland and Woolf** employ only 225 Catholics out of a 3,000 workforce (7.5%) at their giant shipyard. In 1911 the percentage is 7.6% (518 out of 6,809).

Come on lads— let's drive those Fenians out of the shipyard!

In Belfast you get labour conditions the like of which you get in no other town, no other city of equal commercial prosperity from John O'Groats to Land's End or from the Atlantic to the North Sea. It is maintained by an exceedingly simple device... Whenever there is an attempt to root out sweating in Belfast the Orange big drum is beaten...

Ramsay MacDonald, British Labour Party leader 1912.

In 1912 the Liberal Party in England introduces another Home Rule Bill. Alarmed at the prospect of Home Rule by 1914, the Unionists organise.

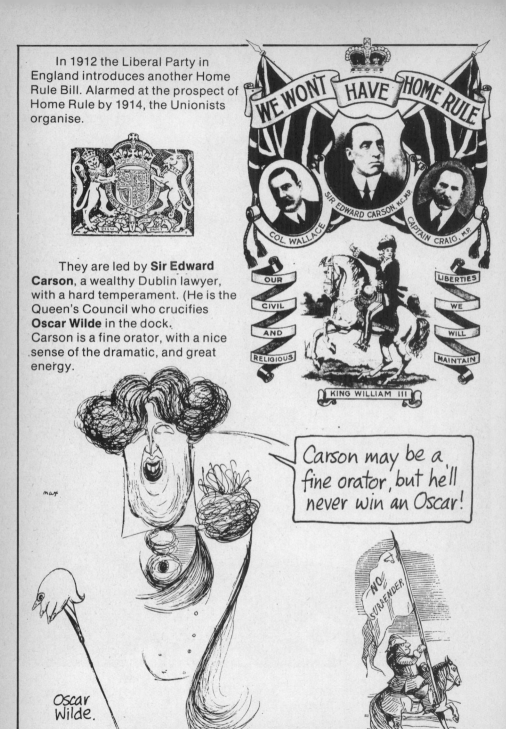

They are led by **Sir Edward Carson**, a wealthy Dublin lawyer, with a hard temperament. (He is the Queen's Council who crucifies **Oscar Wilde** in the dock. Carson is a fine orator, with a nice sense of the dramatic, and great energy.

WE WON'T HAVE HOME RULE

COL. WALLACE

SIR EDWARD CARSON, KC.M.P.

CAPTAIN CRAIG, M.P.

OUR CIVIL AND RELIGIOUS

LIBERTIES WE WILL MAINTAIN

KING WILLIAM III

Carson may be a fine orator, but he'll never win an Oscar!

Oscar Wilde.

NO SURRENDER

At a mass rally of Protestants, on September 28, 1912, he is the first to sign an 'Ulster Solemn League and Covenant'.

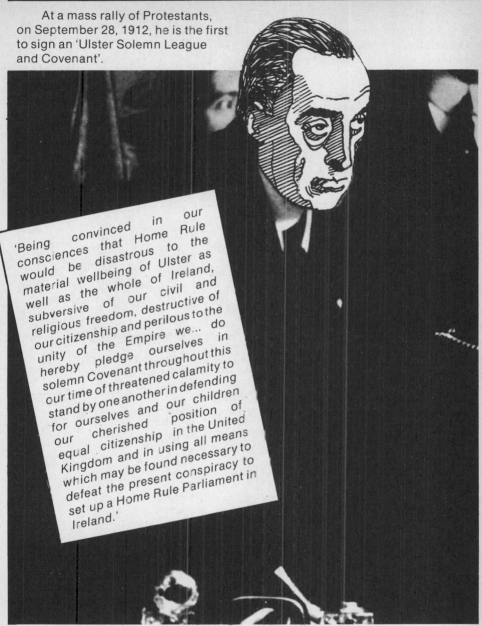

'Being convinced in our consciences that Home Rule would be disastrous to the material wellbeing of Ulster as well as the whole of Ireland, subversive of our civil and religious freedom, destructive of our citizenship and perilous to the unity of the Empire we... do hereby pledge ourselves in solemn Covenant throughout this our time of threatened calamity to stand by one another in defending for ourselves and our children our cherished position of equal citizenship in the United Kingdom and in using all means which may be found necessary to defeat the present conspiracy to set up a Home Rule Parliament in Ireland.'

400,000 sign, some in blood. Often it is signed under duress. Employers intimate that failure to sign may have 'consequences'. Landlords pass 'the List' to tenants: customers do the same to shopkeepers. Workers in the Ulster shipyards who will not sign are designated as 'Papists' — and run off the job.

Major Phillips enjoying himself in Malta.

HENRY JOHN

HAVE YOU EVER been to Malta? Lovely place. Beautiful beaches. I went there last year. Arrived 8 o'clock in the morning. Straight to the beach. Sun beating down. Water glinting. Gorgeous! Set up the deck-chair, slapped on the suntan lotion, got the knotted hankie on the head and settled down to soak it all up, full of poetry and well-being...

Suddenly a familiar voice boomed in my ear. "Henry John!" it said. "Fancy you being here!" And dammit to hell if it wasn't Major Phillips, my ex-boss. "Sure Major," I says, "You've been recommending this here Malta place till us for so long, I thought I'd take a chance on it myself when the oul' compensation came through." He goes there every year, like...

£200 I got, for the mangled hand. I done that in a machine, so I did. £200 and the wee clock for long service.

Major Phillips! Used to be my commandant in the B-Specials too, before they were disbanded, but I refuse to talk about that now, or I'll just get upset. He's in the UDR now of course. Great military man. But not tremendous on personnel relations. "Did you never think of joining up yourself yet, Henry John?" he says. "They said I wasn't suitable sir," I says. Talk about spoiling your holiday!

"Still," he says, "You're a lucky man."

"Pardon?" I says

"You're a lucky man," he says. "Alice Smith, there, she got chewed to death by her machine. Nobody knew till two hours after it happened. Tell me, are you right handed, by any chance, Henry John?"

"No, sir," I says. 'Not any more."

ROSIE

HAVE YOU SEEN that photo of the wee Orangeman standing outside his house? "This We Will Maintain!" he's saying. It's emblazoned across his gable wall along with King Billy on a white horse, and he's all puffed up and bustin' with pride. Two up, two down, no bath, outside toilet *and this he will maintain!*

I tell you what, this I will maintain: there is nothing religious about poverty. There is nothing inherent in a person's beliefs that says he or she has to be economically privileged or discounted. There is no commandment of the Protestant, Catholic, Presbyterian, Muslim, Jewish or any other faith that says, "Thou Shalt Be Better Off Than Anybody Else, and Furthermore Thou Shalt Get All The Good Jobs." So don't talk to me about religion.

Talk to me about money, talk to me about power, talk to me about getting people to do things — one religion is as handy as the next.

And I'll tell you something else. Religion may be the opiate of the people, or religion may be a comfort to the oppressed, but ignorance! Ignorance is the hemlock of the people. The hemlock and the downfall and the ruination and the paralysis of the people!

Does that wee man *know* that King Billy didn't do it for him? That he did it to spite Louis Quatorze of France? That he won the Boyne alright but by Aughrim he was long gone outa that? King Billy of "glorious and immortal memory" was like our Bernie on her holidays. She had Lloret de Mar devastated in a fortnight. "Hit and run," she says. "Calella next year!" The boul' King Billy went to France.

In 1913, the Unionists raise a body of 80,000 Ulster 'Volunteers', armed by the gentry and the Orange Lodges. The Ulster Volunteer Force threaten armed revolt in the event of a Dublin parliament being imposed on Ulster.

Edward Carson he had a cat
And it sat upon the fender.
Every time he pulled its tail
It shouted—

NO SURRENDER!

—so the Prime Minister said 'You realise you can be shot for mutiny Captain?' and I said 'Oh yes?' and then he started to talk about the weather!

OFFICERS MESS

Mutiny!

The depth of British officer-class sympathy with Carson is demonstrated in 1914, when the Government warns officers at the Curragh Camp to prepare to put down a UVF insurrection. 57 officers tender their resignations, and many others threaten to do the same. It is a clear case of mutiny.

The Government capitaulates. It announces it has no intention of 'coercing' Ulster.

the Nationalists

From 1900 *Sinn Fein* grows. It has 'Fenian influences for ts father and the Gaelic revival for its mother'. Sinn Fein — roughly translated — means 'Ourselves Alone'. The emphasis is on self-reliance. Its leader, Arthur Griffith declares it should have nothing to do with the Imperial Parliament in Britain.

> Ourselves alone!

The Irish Republican Brotherhood is still active, and plans to establish the Irish Republic by physical force. Its motto is Wolfe Tone's — 'To break the connection with England'.

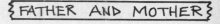

I have found out a gift
   for my Erin *
A gift that will surely
   content her —
Sweet pledge of love
   so endearing!
Five millions of bullets
   I've sent her.
[Freeman's Journal: Dublin 1827.]
* Ireland

There is yet another republican current. Revolutionary socialism. Its most powerful theoretician and organiser is **James Connolly**.

Connolly was born in 1868, in Edinburgh, the son of a poor emigrant Irish family. As a child he works as a printer's 'devil'. At 14 he joins the British Army — and serves in Ireland. He manages to educate himself and becomes: 'a very encyclopaedia of statistical facts and figures and of Marxist economics, a victimised industrial martyr even then...'

In 1896 Connolly founds the Irish Socialist Republican Party. Its programme links the political and national struggle, echoing Marx:

The Irish question is not simply a national question. Ruin or revolution is the watchword... The private ownership by a class of the land and instruments of production, distribution and exchange is opposed to this vital principle of justice, and is the fundamental basis of all oppression, national, political and social.

In an article on 'Nationalism and Socialism' Connolly warns:

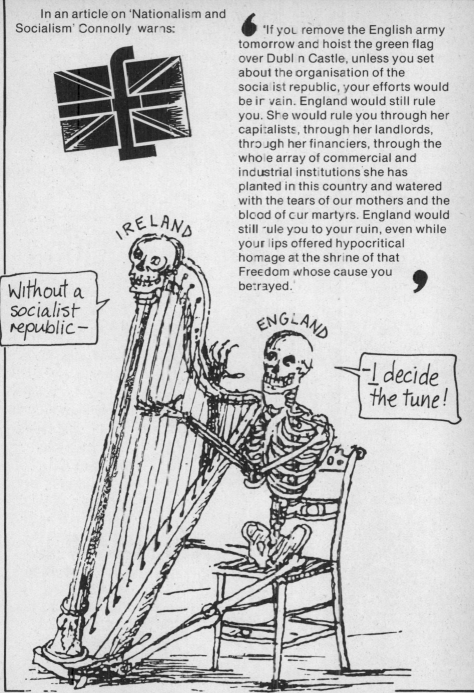

'If you remove the English army tomorrow and hoist the green flag over Dublin Castle, unless you set about the organisation of the socialist republic, your efforts would be in vain. England would still rule you. She would rule you through her capitalists, through her landlords, through her financiers, through the whole array of commercial and industrial institutions she has planted in this country and watered with the tears of our mothers and the blood of our martyrs. England would still rule you to your ruin, even while your lips offered hypocritical homage at the shrine of that Freedom whose cause you betrayed.'

Like **Lenin** and **Trotsky**, Connolly is a member of the Second International.

Connolly founds a newspaper, the *Workers Republic*. He takes part in the centenary celebration of the 1798 rising, and organises opposition to the Boer War (taking the Boers' side, of course).

Connolly seems to be a decent fellow!

A decent fellow, Leon, is one who makes a revolution!

Trotsky.

Lenin.

Left: Lord Kitchener suppresses the rebellious South African colonists.

Connolly is a republican...

He campaigns against the Diamond Jubilee of Queen Victoria.

STUFF THE JUBILEE

He can, however, find work only as a labourer. Poverty forces him to emigrate to America in 1903. He becomes organiser of the anarcho-syndicalist Industrial Workers of the World (IWW), nicknamed the 'Wobblies' because of the way its Chinese members pronounce the 'W's'.

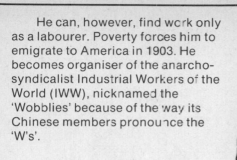

I don't stand here for the liberty to **organise**, dammit!

Connolly returns to Ireland in 1910, as industrial organiser of **Jim Larkin's** Irish Transport and General Workers' Union.

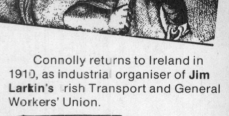

Have you heard— Connolly's back!

Down tools, boys!

Industrial struggle

In 1908 Protestant and Catholics unite in a great strike in Belfast. Dockers, carters and coal workers come out for a wage claim and the right to organise — as does the police, the Royal Irish Constabulary. A Protestant trade unionist says:

Men of all creeds will stand together in fighting the common enemy who denies the right of workers to a fair wage!

Damn! They're **united**! That takes the biscuit!

The Government brings in troops: the police RIC militants are posted to far-away areas. The dockers are defeated by their English leadership's betrayal. Other workers win major concessions.

In 1913 the richest man in Dublin leads an attack on the ITGWU. **WM Murphy** is chairman of the Employers' Federation — and a Home Ruler. He denounces the union through his mouthpiece, the *Independent*. Larkin calls for a <u>boycott</u> of the paper.

Murphy retaliates by calling for all bosses to bar ITGWU workes, he sacks all trade unionists from the trams, and locks them out at his giant Jacob's biscuit factory.

The strikes spread. The workers face an alliance of Loyalist police, Orange magistrates, Nationalist bosses, Catholic church officials, and Dublin Castle.

English and Scottish trade unionists and socialists organise food ships for the strikers and accommodation for their children. (Two are charged with 'kidnapping' by Catholic priests.) 20,000 jobless tramp Dublin's streets.

Six months' hunger drives the strikers back. Connolly and Larkin are jailed. Connolly goes on hunger strike and Dublin Castle releases him. He immediately sets about organising a Citizen Army — to defend workers against the forces of the state.

Below: Citizen Army on parade.

As a counter to the UVF, nationalist forces set up a National Volunteer Force, which soon has over 100,000 members. In July 1914, the NVF obtains 1100 rifles — and starts to march on Dublin. they are intercepted by police — but vanish with the guns.

HALT! What have you got in those boxes?

AH.....

PLAYING FOR TIME

Oh – THOSE boxes – ah, well, some biscuits for my mother, and I heard that Mrs O'Connolly's goat's got a cold and I like your uniforms – and there's a good filum on at –

In 1914 disaster engulfs Europe. Britain enters the Great War.

War

The war of nation against nation in the interest of royal freebooters, and cosmopolitan thieves, is a thing accursed...

Connolly

Over 150,000 Irishmen fought in the war. Carson, who is a member of the British war cabinet, offers 35,000 UVF members to the war effort. Lord Kitchener agrees to the name 'Ulster' being included in all the Loyalist units. The British soon ensure that the Volunteers seal their Covenant in blood — on the Somme. The 36th (Ulster) Division loses 5,500 men in the first two days of the offensive. The 'Shankill Boys', who advance into No Man's Land shouting 'No Surrender!' and 'Remember 1690!' are left with 70 men out of 700. There is no celebration of the 'Glorious Twelfth' in 1916 in Belfast. Blinds are drawn and processions are cancelled.

The Real Thing

A Story of Kitchener's Lads at the Front

There is a general sympathy throughout Ireland for Britain. The proportion of recruits per head of population is much higher in Nationalist Ireland than in 'Ulster'. The fact is concealed by the British, who disperse these volunteers in various brigades, with no distinctive identity, but with proportional casualties...

Conscription is not introduced in Ireland.

Many leading republicans support the war, like **John Redmond**, leader of the IRB. Connolly's paper jingles:

Full steam ahead
    John Redmond said
That everything was well chum;
  Home Rule will come
    when we are dead
  And buried out in Belgium.

Men of the 36TH.

In the first two days of the Battle of the Somme the 36TH (Ulster) Division loses 5,500 men ...

YOU

In 1915 the body of the old Fenian **O'Donovan Rossa** is brought from America for burial in Dublin. Padraig Pearse makes an inspiring graveside oration:

Life springs from death; and from the graves of patriot men and women spring living nations. The Defenders of this realm have worked well in secret and in the open. They think that they have pacified Ireland. They think that they have purchased half of us and intimidated the other half. They think that they have foreseen everything, think that they have provided against everything; but the fools, the fools, the fools! They have left us our Fenian dead, and while Ireland holds these graves, Ireland unfree shall never be at peace...

A volley is fired over Rossa's grave.

James Connolly decides that an insurrection must be attempted — with the cooperation of the IRB if possible, but if necessary with his Citizen Army alone. The date is set: <u>Easter Sunday, 1916.</u> **Roger Casement**, an ex-member of the British consular service, is in Germany attempting to get arms for the republican movement, and raise a brigade among Irish prisoners of war to fight the British in Ireland. The Germans agree to send an arms ship with 20,000 rifles, ammunition and 10 machine guns.

Hearing of the imminent rising, Casement panics. He fears it is premature. But he manages to persuade the Germans to send the arms ship.

Roger Casement

When the ship arrives in Tralee Bay (having evaded the British blockade) there is no-one to meet it. The ship is captured by the Royal Navy, but scuttled by its captain in Queenstown Bay.

Casement lands from a German submarine at Banna Strand, County Kerry.

CASEMENT LANDS—

It is Good Friday, but as far as Casement is concerned, it is not so good. His dinghy overturns. Wet and exhausted, he is captured by police.

—AND IS CAPTURED.

Solid land showed about him; there were stunted fir trees, steeply sloping fields green with thin grass; there were even sheep placidly grazing. "Ship ahoy!" yelled a figure and waved what was apparently a shepherd's plaid. "Land ahoy!" answered Rex

the Easter Rising

Shortly before noon on Easter Monday (the date has been changed) 150 members of the Citizen Army and Volunteers march off from the ITGWU's Liberty Hall in Dublin. They take possession of the Post Office and hoist the green, white and orange tricolour.

An abortive attack is made on Dublin Castle. The Rising has begun.

On the steps of the Post Office Pacraig Pearse reads the Proclamation of the Irish Republic to a bemused crowd.

...The Provisional Government of the Irish Republic salutes the Citizens of Dublin on the momentous occasion of the proclamation of a SOVEREIGN INDEPENDENT IRISH STATE now in the course of being established by Irishmen in arms... We have lived to see the Irish Republic proclaimed. May we live to establish it firmly, and may our children and our children's children enjoy the happiness and prosperity which freedom will bring...

EH?

The authorities are taken by surprise, despite reports from agents that a rising is expected. There are outbreaks by rebels in Galway — under Liam Mellows — and Wexford. The Government soon retaliates with troops and artillery. The gunboat *Helga,* stationed on the River Liffey, lobs shells into the Post Office. There is heavy fighting, but one by one the rebel strongholds fall. Pearse surrenders on the Saturday. Other centres — including St Stephen's Green; where the redoubtable **Countess Markiewicz** is second-in-command — give in the next day.

INSIDE THE POST OFFICE AFTER THE RISING...

The middle of Dublin lies in ruins. Fifty-six rebels and 130 British are dead. Two hundred civilians die: casualties total 3,000.

At first public reaction is hostile to the rebels. The authorities take a savage vengeance. Day after day sees executions of rebel prisoners. Pearse is shot. In his death cell, he writes 'We shall be remembered by posterity and blessed by unborn generations'.

Connolly, who has had a foot amputated, is executed tied to a chair. 'He was very brave and cool,' said the chaplain. (On Easter Monday Connolly had confided to a comrade: 'We are going out to be slaughtered'.)

Below: Women outside Mountjoy Prison, Dublin, await execution of 19-year-old student.

Public opinion begins to change as the executions continue. It dawns that Connolly and his comrades have through their sacrifice shown the way to loosen Britain's grip on Ireland. (The change in popular attitude comes too late to save Roger Casement, who is hanged in Pentonville in August.)

Lenin writes in defence of the Rising:

To imagine that a social revolution is conceivable without revolts of small nations... to imagine that is tantamount to repudiating social revolution.

The misfortune of the Irish is that they rose prematurely, when the European revolt of the proletariat* had not yet matured. Capitalism is not so harmoniously built that the various springs of rebellion can immediately merge into one, of their own accord, without reverses and defeats.

* working class

Connolly himself had already summed up the matter:

You never know if the time is ripe until you try. If you succeed the time is ripe. If not, then it was not ripe.

In 1918 **Lloyd George** attempts to introduce conscription in Ireland.

The Irish MPs go 'Sinn Fein' and walk out of the Commons. In the General Election of 1918 the Sinn Fein republicans sweep the board, winning 73 seats (36 of the successful candidates being in gaol).

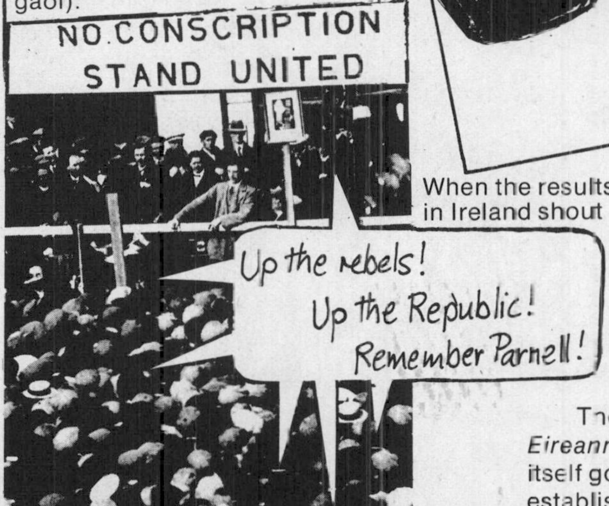

NO CONSCRIPTION
STAND UNITED

YOUR COUNTRY NEEDS
"YOU
DEAD"

When the results are announced crowds in Ireland shout

Up the rebels!
Up the Republic!
Remember Parnell!

the Dail

Those elected form the *Dail Eireann* (Irish Assembly). It declares itself government of the 'Republic established in Easter Week'. The Dail, with its own courts, and funds from the public (the 'Loan') comes under attack from the British, who raid its premises and arrest its leading figures.

The Volunteers — by now popularly known as the Irish Republican Army (IRA) ambushes troops and police. The fighting escalates. The British introduce a curfew — and the infamous 'Black and Tans', so called because of the odd mix of RIC black and army khaki in their uniforms.

The 'Tans' are openly terrorist. Many of them are ex-criminals, released early on condition of joining up. A historian remarks that they have 'exactly the same social composition as that of the ... SS face of Nazi terrorism'.

Black and Tans: note the steel cage for protection against missiles.

The Tans carry out a systematic campaign of murder, rape, beatings, looting and burning. The IRA — now with the support of most of the population — fights back with what weapons it has.

1920 sees a massive anti-Catholic pogrom in Belfast.

'The decision to expel the Nationalist Workmen from the Queen's Island shipyard followed on a dinner-hour meeting of Unionist workers'.
Manchester Guardian

Crowds attack Catholic areas.

The pogrom is led by 'Special Constables', recruited among unemployed Orangemen. In the first assault 22 die. The riot spreads to Lisburn. In Belfast 9,000 Catholics lose their jobs: 30,000 are made destitute. As the riots end 62 lie dead; there are thousands more injured.

In August the Mayor of Cork, arrested for participating in an illegal Sinn Fein Court, goes on hunger strike against his two year sentence in Brixton gaol. Seventy-four days later **Terence McSwiney** dies. He says:

The contest on our side is not one of rivalry or vengeance but of endurance. It is not those who can inflict the most but those who can suffer the most that will conquer...

Black and Tans open fire on a crowd at a football match in Dublin and kill 12. Edward Carson remarks that Catholics have:

...only to take an oath of allegiance to the King, and pledge their loyalty to the Empire, and the trouble would cease immediately.

The Black and Tans burn down the centre of Cork, following the death of 17 of their number in an IRA ambush. The 'Auxies' (Auxiliaries) carry out reprisals, as one of their officers explains:

'Talk about Western films, they weren't in it! The Black and Tans used to carry a holster on the thigh with a revolver... hanging from the ring of the revolver they had a half-burnt cork, and they used to say

If you ambush us, then you know what's going to happen; Half of Cork has been burnt and be careful or we might burn down your place!

ULP!

But the British are losing their grip. The Orange enclave in the North excepted, the terror has polarised the whole population against the British — and for a republic. The government opens negotiations with **Eamonn De Valera**, who speaks for the Dail — and with **Michael Collins** (who has been on the run with £10,000 on his head).

The British, with their centuries of experience in similar situations, outwit the Irish. The 'Treaty' of December 1921 is signed.

The Treaty satisfies no-one. It gives Ireland 'Dominion' status (like Australia and Canada). But it also requires an Irish government to sign an oath of 'Allegiance' to the British crown.

Worst of all, it partitions Ireland. Six counties of a diminished 'Ulster' — Londonderry, Antrim, Fermanagh, Down, Tyrone and Armagh — are to have separate 'self-determination' from the 26 counties of the 'Free State' in the South.

You've agreed to this partition Michael — but mark my words — it's going to cause a lot of trouble — because I don't!

Eamonn De Valera   Michael Collins

Collins reflects:

'When you have sweated, toiled, had mad dreams, hopeless nightmares, you find yourselves in London's streets, cold and dark in the night air... Think — what have I got for Ireland? Something which she has wanted these past seven hundred years. Will anyone be satisfied at the bargain? Will anyone? I tell you this — early this morning I signed my death warrant. I thought at the time how old, how ridiculous — a bullet may just as well have done the job five years ago.'

Collins is right. Even Carson — inveterate enemy of a British surrender of Ireland — is shocked by partition. He retires from politics.

The Treaty splits the nationalist movement down the middle and starts a Civil war between Pro and Anti Treatyites.

Winston Churchill, colonial secretary, writes to his Dublin agent:

> You should do everything in your power to persuade Mr Collins to draw arms from the British Government which has a large surplus. I am quite ready to continue the flow of arms to trustworthy Free State troops...

Michael Collins.

Churchill.

The Civil War is a struggle, remembered even today with bitterness, dividing families and comrades who had given their all in the movement for independence.

The Free State, who support the Treaty, face intransigent 'Republicans' — who include **De Valera, Liam Mellows** and **Liam Lynch** (who leads the irregular soldiers of the IRA). Mellows and Lynch die after capture whilst 'trying to escape'. Collins dies in a republican ambush.

My grandfather **built** this state!

HENRY JOHN

LET ME TELL YOU about politicians.

Politicians think they can pick you up and drop you as the fancy takes them. Off you go, boys, and fight this wee war for us... "What for?"... Freedom and democracy!... "What about our freedom? What about our democracy?"... Oh no. Cloth ears, hear no evil, see no evil, bloody shower of monkeys, politicians are.

My grandfather *built* this State. My grandfather drilled and patrolled and kept anti-social hours for this State. His teeth were grit, his bayonet fixed and his heart was set on it. And when democracy had been established, the A and C Specials were disbanded and what had himself and his colleagues to show? Not a fart's worth of gratitude, nor a penny's worth of pay-off money, and this a week before Christmas!

Of course your politician has got to be a bit of a wheeler-dealer, eye on the main chance, upstairs-downstairs-in-me-Lady's-chamber sort of a character. But enough is enough is it not?

O'Neill failed, Chichester-Clarke failed, Faulkner failed, Heath failed, Wilson failed, the list goes on. Nobody can remember what Atkins did, and before Airey Neave got a chance to do nothing he got blew up for it — when will they learn? As soon as power-sharing comes to the fore, down goes the government. Because you cannot argue with what happens in the street.

We never had this trouble with Brookborough.

ROSIE

MY HUSBAND'S dead. Aye. Charlie was his name. See my neighbour, but! "I suppose youse all regret that fight I heard youse at that final morning," she says...

I remember it well. "*Tactics!*" our Michael was saying. "Tactics is one thing. Defeatism is another!" — "I'm not talking about defeatism!" says Charlie, "But you can't coerce a million screaming Prods into a Republic they don't *want!*" — "Coerce!" says Michael. "I'll tell you where the coercion is — it's here and now where there's half a million of us has been coerced into an artificial statelet *we* never wanted. And the means of that there coercion is a standing army supporting the British presence here. Now if you *remove* that presence, till your border shrinks back and back till it falls into the sea, where's the *coercion* in that, eh? If you call that *coercion*, you need your head examined — it's no wonder you can't get a bloody job!"

Out of work for ten years...

Well I can't abide disrespect in a child, so I was off! "You don't know the half of what that man has been through to keep this family fed and clothed! There's women in this street who have to steal the house-keeping out of their man's pocket when he comes home plastered on pay night, or they'd never see it at all. I have *never* had to do that! Your father comes home here, hands me over my money and sits down to tea with his family. *Then* he goes out and gets plastered!" I said. (Well I can't resist a laugh!)

They stabbed that man 97 times. Then they strung him up by his ankles like a bloody carcass.

"No," I says. "I do not indeed regret that there. I regret, however, the fact that my husband lived and died and never had a decent house to live in. And this here is the irony of it! Do you know what his trade was, but? He was a bricklayer. Aye. Been out of work for ten years! That's what I regret."

Seventy-seven republican prisoners are executed by Free State forces, who gradually gain the upper hand. The Civil War is won as the IRA runs out of weapons and ammunition, and a war-weary population yearns for peace. With victory partition becomes established fact. A 'Boundary Commission', run by the Orange Order, confirms the status of the North as British, with its own semi-devolved 'parliament' (run by the Orange Order).

In 1927, De Valera, who survived the Civil War, caves in — and takes the 'Oath' as a member of the Dail. He founds a new party, *Fianna Fail* ('Soldiers of Destiny').

De Valera

All Ireland is laid waste in the great depression of the 1930's. The 26 Counties are used to it being under-capitalised. But in the shipyards and mills of the North a remarkable thing happens as layoffs and closures mount. Protestant and Catholic workers unite against the casual cruelty of the dole queue and the workhouse, which still operates in the hands of Poor Law Guardians:

Unity!

In October 1932 tens of thousands of unemployed march demanding 'Work — not Charity'. **Saidie Patterson**, union organiser, remembers:

'...when we got outside the workhouse we sat down. It was a step in the right direction. *The Falls and the Shankill* (the two main Catholic and Protestant streets in Belfast respectively) *united*.'

TIGER BAY

ARDOYNE NEW LODGE

SHANKILL UNITY

BALLYMURHY LOWER FALLS

TURF LODGE SANDY ROW MARKETS

east belfast

city centre

BELFAST

ANDERSONTOWN

LENADOON

:::: Catholic Areas
///// Protestant Areas

110

United! But not for long. RUC attacks on Catholic areas follow a hurried raising of Poor Law rates.

There is a barrage of sectarian speeches by Unionist politicians. Sir Basil Brooke (later Prime Minister in the North) says at the 12 July gala in 1933:

Catholics were out to destroy Ulster in all their might and power!

BASIL BROOKE.

In 1935 there is sectarian rioting again: 11 Catholics die in the 6 counties...

Meanwhile De Valera wins a majority in the Dail. In 1932 he immediately abolishes the 'Oath of Allegiance' and releases his old anti-Treaty comrades from prison. Britain announces 'Economic War' to discipline Ireland. It is a big flop. A deal is signed. It sets the seal on the complete independence of the 26 Counties.

THE 'ECONOMIC WAR'.

the new Constitution

In 1937 De Valera introduces a new Irish Constitution. It is nothing like the workers' state envisaged by James Connolly or his comrades. It has a strong Catholic Church slant, recognising '... the special position of the Holy Apostolic and Roman Church as the Guardian of the Faith professed by the great majority of the citizens'. It defends freedom of religion, but recognises 'the Family as the natural primary and fundamental unit group of society'.

Thou Shalt not kill

'No law,' it announces, 'shall be enacted providing for the grant of a dissolution of a marriage.'

That's bad – but maybe I can be dissolute *inside* marriage!

The Constitution is a gift to the Protestant ruling bigots of the 6 Counties, who point out its medieval, Vatican-inspired, defects. Where is the non-sectarian state promised by the republicans?

I **told** you the **Pope** would take over the 26 Counties in the South!

By the way, what's a 'Taioseach'?

A bad pain – just like a Prime minister!

The Constitution has other contradictions. It maintains that the government of the South still has jurisdiction over the North:

'The national territory consists of the whole island of Ireland, its islands and territorial seas.' (Article 2)

The Constitution sets up a Dail (parliament), a Senate (on the American model) and Taoiseach appointed by the elected party majority in the Dail via a president.

De Valera becomes Taoiseach. Like Michael Collins before him, he turns against his old comrades — and cracks down on the IRA.

The traditionalist rump of the IRA, Japanese-style, refuse to admit that the war is lost and shoot Irish policemen (Gardai).

The English hangman, Pierrepoint, is invited over to carry out executions. Internment camps are opened.

PIERREPOINT.

Courage my son — you are being hanged for Ireland!

An IRA raid on the magazine fort in Phoenix Park in Dublin in 1939 enrages the government. The IRA steals most of the country's ammunition.

The anti-IRA crackdown intensifies. At Curragh internment camp warders savagely beat up dozens of 'rioting' IRA prisoners. One is shot. When his lawyer enquires why he has been shot in the back the inquest is closed '...within seconds'.

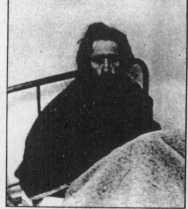

At the Portlaoise prison, in pursuit of withdrawn 'political status', IRA prisoners go 'on the blanket' — refusing to wear prison-issue clothing — for the duration of the war.

During the 30s, as in other countries, a fascist party has grown up in Ireland. It is known as the 'Blue-Shirts'.

There is sporadic conflict with Irish republicans and socialists in the pre-war years. The fascists call themselves the 'Army Comrades Association'.

Not that book, you fool!

WHAT DO YOU DO IF A NAZI THROWS A GRENADE AT YOU?

PULL THE PIN OUT AND THROW IT BACK!

War

When the long-expected war finally breaks out, despite Ireland's declared neutrality, popular sympathy is with the Allies. Thousands volunteer and die in the war against fascism. In the North 38,000 fight; 7,500 die. Old guard republicans, however, maintain the old attitude, 'England's Difficulty is Ireland's Opportunity'. Britain secretly considers an invasion of Ireland to cover their Atlantic flank against German influence.

ENGLAND'S DIFFICULTY IS IRELAND'S OPPORTUNITY

DEAD DEAD

WAR

The Nazi **La Hous** complains at his trial in Nuremburg in 1946 that:

"We got no satisfaction with the IRA because those fellows were concerned with their own ends!"

-That's because the IRA are all Jews!

De Valera introduces a Teason Act and an Offences Against the State Act. These acts are purportedly to deal with foreign agents. But the acts are used against the IRA. The Offences Against the State Act, with its powers of detention without trial is still in frequent use (as your author has found out) against militant republicans.

GARDA SÍOCHÁNA

INFORMATION FOR PERSONS IN CUSTODY

Under the Offences Against the State Act, 1939, a member of the Garda Síochána is authorised to take, or cause to be taken, the fingerprints of any person arrested under Section 30 of that Act. In any other case, a member of the Garda Síochána may take the fingerprints of a person in custody in a Garda Station, with his or her consent.

On the night of April 15 1941 the Germans blitz Belfast. The fire brigades of Dublin and Dun Laoghaire (Dunleary) race North across the border to fight the fires raging after the incendiary attack. It is a symbolic — and practical — demonstration of the South's solidarity and national unity with the North.

ABOVE: BELFAST AFTER THE BLITZ.
BELOW: BELFAST TODAY.

BRITISH SHIPBUILDING LEADS THE WORLD

British Achievements Speak for Britain

The British government introduces conscription in Britain — but not in the six counties.

HENRY JOHN

DOESN'T IT make you wonder, the way people never learn? The first time I saw Lally McGovern with a black face was the night of the Blitz, 1941. Poor Lally was so heartscared all alone in the wee back kitchen of the corner shop there, that she took a notion into her head to hide under the table. (Safe as houses as the man said when he invented the neutron bomb). Well, what would you have, a bomb goes off two streets away, all the soot falls down Lally's chimney and when I'm sent over to see is she alright, there's Lally still under the table looking like a golliwog.

Lally looking like a golliwog.

The second time I saw Lally McGovern with a black face was in 1971 when the IRA was trying to blast us all into the Republic. Where was Lally? Underneath the table in the wee back kitchen of the corner shop. Boom! Up goes the Masonic Lodge, down comes the soot, in I go and there's our Lally under the table looking like another golliwog.

Lally looking like another golliwog

See if there's a nuclear war? There she'll be, under the table again, likely as not, if God spares her. Only this time it'll be her goes up the chimney and ends up stuck to the soot!

And incidentally of course, nuclear holocaust is exactly what you're asking for if you remove that border. Have you never heard of the North Atlantic Treaty Organization? Aay home and read your Bible, as the man said! Northern Ireland still, as ever, guards the back door of Britain, lest you forget. I mean, get it straight, who is sponging on who here?

ROSIE

HAVE I TOLD YOU about the cousin who won't venture north? The cousin Donal? he lives in Drogheda, not 60 miles away. So I asked him about it.

"The air's not so fresh," he said.

"Away to hell," I said, the Parish Priest has your head filled with nonsense."

"I might get shot when they hear the accent."

"You just load your pockets up with them strong Free State fags, son," I says, "You'll find the natives very friendly."

"And then there's the mountains," he said. (Would you credit it!)

"We're not talking about Cisalpine Gaul," I says, "The only thing separates your part of the world from my part of the world is a few wee drumlin hills long since drained and put into good Protestant order by Scots settlers in the year dot minus three and conveniently traversed by the main Belfast/Dublin arterial road, thanks to the splendid auspices of various county councils north and south, a fine example of cross border collaboration and a road which not only *did* manage to meet in the middle at the appointed place, but travels in both directions, so you *can* get back, you know."

Couldn't shift him. It transpired that he'd been once before and didn't take to it.

August 15th 1941, the night of the Blitz. He was one of the Drogheda fire-fighting team that screamed up north to assist. It was a desperate journey, he said, and when they got there the atmosphere was wicked, smoke and smog and bombs and blasts and God knows what.

Swore he'd never go back.

Parish priest filling somebody's head with a lot of nonsense..

100,000 are made homeless by the Nazi raids. 942 die. A hundred thousand people camp up Cave Hill, in the suburbs, at night. The Independent Unionist MP for the Protestant Shankill Road remarks anxiously :

The Catholics and Protestants are going up there, mixed, and they are <u>talking to each other</u>. They are sleeping in the same sheugh, below the same tree or in the same barn. They all say the same thing, that —

–The Government is no good !!

Evacuees from Belfast, May 1941

Irish capitalists did well out of the war. Between 1938 and 1946 the money value of bank deposits rose by 103 per cent.

At Easter 1949, following an inconclusive election in 1948, a Republic is declared. The Treaty has been forgotten — it is no longer an issue. But the Irish economy is in a terrible mess, decapitalised and backward.

THE REPUBLIC.

408,766 emigrate between 1951 and 1961.

Emigration

'...the small farmers lost their grip on the soil. The mid-twentieth century witnessed clearances as decisive as the mid-nineteenth. But there were no crowbar brigades. The compulsion was economic and the people left quietly. Whole families departed and some western townlands were left with scarcely an inhabited house... The legatees of a culture two thousand years old flooded into the social deserts of the English midlands where life normally consisted of work, worry and drugged sleep and where the sole amenity was drink.'

T.A. JACKSON : HISTORIAN.

Mrs Sharkey, of Donegal.

That unless there's a spurt in procreation
We can bid goodbye to the Irish nation;
It's growing smaller year by year —
And don't pretend that's not your affair.
Between death and war and ruin and pillage
The land is like a deserted village....

from The Midnight Court : Brian Merriman (1747-1805)

The IRA, too, is in crisis. In October 1954, Standing Order No 8 belatedly redefines its aims:

'Volunteers are strictly forbidden to take any militant actions against 26-County forces under any circumstances...'

'...arms are for use against the British Forces of Occupation only.'

Lay down your arms!

Between 1956 and 1962, an abortive 'Border' campaign by the IRA is directed against the authorities in the North, in the shape of attacks on the RUC. It fails to win popular support. The government in the 26 Counties. sets up a Special Criminal Court to deal with IRA suspects.

"How to sleep with your gun."

Brendhan Behan's *Borstal Boy* is written about his experiences as a political prisoner in England, following an equally abortive bombing campaign in Britain in the mid 50s.

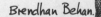

Brendhan Behan.

The economic crisis worsens. In 1965...

Hello! I'm Captain Terence O'Neil, Prime Minister of Northern Ireland. Here in the North
- Unemployment is 4 times the British average.
- Wages are 78% of Britain's.
- 22% of houses have no flush toilet.
- 19·3% of houses have no piped water!

Good morning! I'm Sean Lemass, Prime Minister of the South! We have all the same problems, so we're going to **invite in** foreign capital on favourable terms! Favourable, that is, to the foreign capital, not you peasants!

Welcome
to Europe's fastest-growing business location

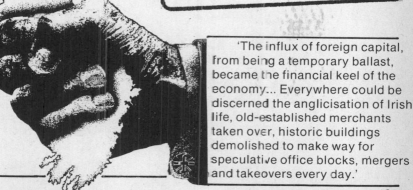

'The influx of foreign capital, from being a temporary ballast, became the financial keel of the economy... Everywhere could be discerned the anglicisation of Irish life, old-established merchants taken over, historic buildings demolished to make way for speculative office blocks, mergers and takeovers every day.'

In 1962, the IRA appears to have given up the ghost, when its Publicity Bureau announces:

'The Leadership of the Resistance Movement has ordered the termination of "The Campaign of Resistance to British Occupation"... all arms and other materials have been dumped and all full-time active service volunteers have been withdrawn.'

There is a gradual rebirth of Irish socialism. Belfast Trades Council holds a conference in 1967. Older Catholic workers tell their Protestant brothers and sisters what it is like to be second-class citizens. A programmed of democratic demands is drawn up.

A spectre is once again haunting the 6 Counties: the spectre of Catholic/Protestant unity.

The 'Orange card' is played again. In the form, this time, of the Knave of Hearts: the Reverend **Ian Kyle Paisley**.

Watch the Jews... Israel is on the way back to favour... Watch the Papist Rome rising to a grand crescendo with the Communists... The Reds are on the march... They are heading for an alliance against the return of the Lord Jesus Christ....*

IAN PAISLEY.

Paisley is no Edward Carson. Carson was a High Tory, a member of the World War I War Cabinet. Paisley appeals instead to last-ditch reaction — small shopkeepers, unemployed Protestants desperate for work, those who fear that their jobs and homes are threatened by competition from Catholics. Paisley draws on the sectarian politics of the gutter.

'The Big Man', as Paisley is called is the authentic voice of the poorer, working-class Protestants. His politics express their self-righteousness, paranoia — and taste for sectarian violence.

BENITO MUSSOLINI.

129

* from the Protestant Telegraph, Paisley's paper.

Civil Rights

In 1968 **Austin Currie** leads a Civil Rights occupation of a council house, at Caledon, County Tyrone which has been allocated to a Protestant over the heads of a long waiting-list of Catholics. The house goes to the 18 year-old unmarried secretary of a local Orange dignitary. Some of the waiting Catholics have as many as 12 children.

HOUSING DEPT. WAIT HERE.

The Civil Rights movement mushrooms. It exposes an astonishing level of discrimination and gerrymandering. Derry (Londonderry to loyalists), for instance, with a population of 36,000 Catholics and 17,000 Protestants, returns a safe Protestant electoral majority.

It demands:

- ONE MAN ONE VOTE.
- REMOVAL OF GERRYMANDERED BOUNDARIES.
- LAWS TO END DISCRIMINATION IN LOCAL GOVERNMENT.
- ALLOCATION OF HOUSING ON A POINTS SYSTEM.
- REPEAL OF THE SPECIAL POWERS ACT.
- DISBANDING OF THE 'B' SPECIALS.

1968

LA LUTTE CONTINUE

In August 1968, the Eventful year, the Civil Rights Association marches 2,500 strong from Coalisland to Dungannon, protesting at local housing policies. The CRA follows it up with a march in Derry — banned by the authorities. The Unionists are outraged. William Craig, Stormont's Home Affairs Minister, turns the RUC on the marchers. Seventy-seven civilians are wounded — and 11 police. TV film of RUC brutality shocks viewers with its scenes of savage beatings and water cannon.

Watercannon in use against bystanders in Derry.

A letter to the press observes :

There was no police brutality in Londonderry. Anything meted out was well deserved and those who marched were deliberately seeking trouble.

signed :

'REASONABLE'

People's Democracy is formed by left-wing Civil Rights campaigners. Its members include **Bernadette Devlin** and **Eamonn McCann**. And 15,000 supporters of the Derry Citizens' Action Committee march in the city.

The British Government becomes anxious. It considers repealing part of Northern Ireland's draconian Special Powers Act of 1922.

Bernadette

> This Act gives the Minister of Home Affairs absolute power to arrest people on suspicion of endangering the state and to imprison them indefinitely without trial.

The Act abrogates two-thirds of the provisions of the Universal Declaration of Human Rights.

> —It also empowers him to send police into homes without warrants, impound property, suspend Habeas Corpus and abolish inquests!

SPECIAL POWERS ACT

133

The People's Democracy plan a 'Long March' from Belfast to Derry.

'The march,' recalls Eamonn McCann, turns out to be 'a horrific seventy-three mile trek which dredged to the surface all the accumulated political filth of fifty Unionist years... It was frequently stoned from the fields and attacked by groups of men with clubs. There was no police protection... at Burntollet Bridge a few miles outside Derry, a force of some hundreds, marshalled by members of the 'B' Specials and watched passively by our 'escort' of more than 100 police, attacked with nailed clubs, stones and bicycle chains. Of the 80 who had set out fewer than 30 arrived uninjured.'

Above: Police look on as loyalists attack the march from the fields.

Prime Minister O'Neill denounces the battered marchers:

Enough is enough. We have heard sufficient for now about civil rights. Let us hear a little about civic responsibility!

Fierce rioting in protest breaks out in Derry. The 'B' Specials go berserk. They rampage through Catholic areas singing:

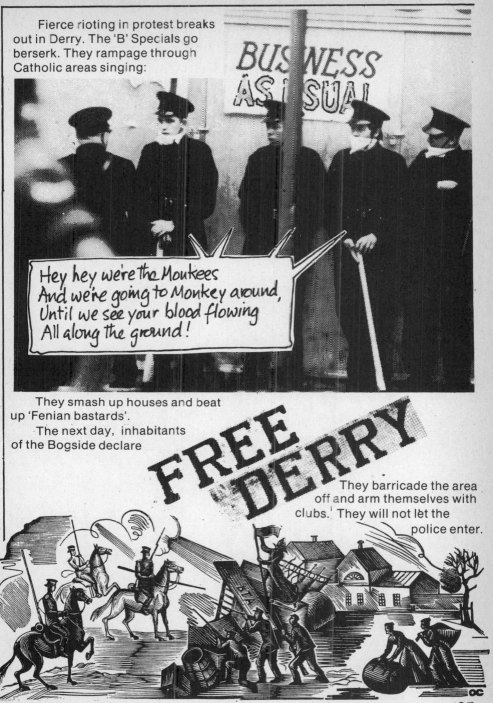

Hey hey we're the Monkees
And we're going to Monkey around,
Until we see your blood flowing
All along the ground!

They smash up houses and beat up 'Fenian bastards'.

The next day, inhabitants of the Bogside declare

FREE DERRY

They barricade the area off and arm themselves with clubs. They will not let the police enter.

On the 12th August, 1969, 15,000 'Apprentice Boys' march to commemorate the breaking of James II's seige of Derry.

Battle of the Bogside

A battle breaks out between Catholic and Protestant youths. The RUC lays seige to the Bogside. This time it is beaten back, defeated, despite the use of CS gas for the first time.

The Prime Minister in the 26 Counties, **Jack Lynch**, is forced by popular concern to declare that

We will not stand by and see innocent people injured and perhaps worse

Lynch.

The Irish Government sets up field hospitals and refugee camps along the border with the 6 Counties. Lynch calls for a UN peacekeeping force to be sent to the North.

On August 14, the British send troops into Derry. At first, they are given a warm welcome:

'The soldiers were welcomed like a liberating army. It seemed to the Catholics that it was a sign of the defeat of the RUC and of the Stormont Government. With the British Army on the streets of Northern Ireland it was felt that the Westminster Government would have to take over,... and the injustices of unionist rule would be removed.'

The British Government predicts that the soldiers will be back in barracks

Bah the wikind !*

* BY THE WEEKEND

The Catholics should know the British Army better than that!

Oliver Cromwell.

The same night Belfast police use armoured cars and machine guns against Catholics, raking houses with gunfire. Ten civilians die and 200 Catholic houses are burned out by Loyalist mobs. Again troops are sent in to the burning city.

The trigger-happy 'B' Specials are disbanded and replaced by the new 'non-sectarian' Ulster Defence Regiment — which immediately recruits the ex-'B' Specials.

Rioting between Protestants and Catholics continues. Bernadette Devlin is jailed in June 1970 for 'riotous behaviour' during the defence of the Bogside.

Bernadette's 'crime' is to be photographed breaking up paving stones to use as weapons against armed police.

the IRA

As the Orange marching season starts, to commemorate the dead of the Battle of the Somme, the <u>UVF</u> launches an armed attack on a tiny Catholic enclave in Belfast, the Short Strand.

' ...the ghetto had been at the mercy of the UVF until the <u>Provisionals</u> stepped out of the shadows to defend their people.'

The gun battle leaves five dead — four of them Protestants. This action earns for the Provisionals political leadership of a sizeable section of Catholics in the North.

The initial welcome for British intervention wears off as the Army ransacks Catholic areas looking for arms. There are sporadic shootings. The Army shoots four dead in a search on the Lower Falls Road. In March 1971 the Provisionals take three soldiers from a Belfast pub and shoot them. The army shoots dead two unarmed rioters in Derry.

Southern Premier JACK LYNCH now says:

> It is for political leaders to govern wisely and justly. I accept the guarantees of the British government that they will do so...

Jack's on our side, Sarge!

Northern Premier O'Neill is succeeded by his cousin Chichester-Clarke. The latter is forced to resign, and is replaced by hard-liner Brian Faulkner.

Brian Faulkner.

'And there was wee Brian Faulkner sitting on a great big chair, looking just as proud as the Pope of Rome himself — and his wee legs were wrapped around the legs of the chair, and I said to my companion, either we're going to have to saw his legs off, or the chair's legs off, to get him off that chair.' Ian Paisley.

139

Paisley's *Protestant Telegraph* exhorts:

The vermin must be suppressed either by internment or effective action by our security forces!

In August 1971 the British introduce internment.

The IRA largely escapes the first swoop, in which 342 are seized. It has advance warning.

Orangemen on the march.

The Catholics rise in open rebellion. Barricades go up again. Catholic councillors resign. 8,000 workers in Derry go on one-day strike, and 26,000 go on rent and rates strike. Fifty 'Moderate' Nationalist MPs leave Stormont and form an 'alternative' assembly at Dungiven.

In the four months after internment, 30 soldiers, 11 RUC and UDR men and 73 civilians die. By December 600 are interned, indefinitely.

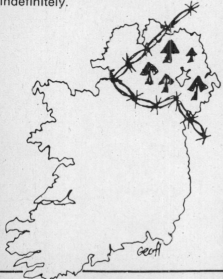

Five years later the European Commission of Human Rights in Strasbourg finds Britain guilty of torturing those seized.

'The interrogation techniques included sensory deprivation — covering the head with a thick black hood; deprivation of sleep for several days; forcing victims to stand against a wall supported only by the fingertips, and subjecting them to continuous 'white noise' from a machine specifically designed to induce disorientation in its victims. Many... were to suffer severe damage as a result, some of them permanently.'

'When I realized I wasn't dead, I cried'.

John McGuffin, in 'THE GUINEA PIGS'

141

The Fenian O'Donovan Rossa, chained in prison in 1869, and forced to eat his food off the floor...

Torture, "ill-treatment", "cruel and degrading treatment", "interrogation": choose any description one wishes; this has been an integral part of the Northern scene since at least 1971. For the crackdown on the Catholic population of the North did not end with internment.

Tim Pat Coogan: 'ON THE BLANKET'.

YOU ARE NOW ENTERING FREE DERRY

If a genuine and serious grievance arose, such as might result from a significant drop in the standard of living, all those who now dissipate their protest over a wide variety of causes might concentrate their efforts and produce a situation which was beyond the power of the police to handle. **Should this happen the army would be required to restore the situation rapidly...**

9mm Browning Pistol.

Brigadier Frank Kitson: 'LOW INTENSITY OPERATIONS'.

The British make extensive use of the Special Air Service (SAS) for undercover work and assassinations. A campaign of 'black propaganda' to discredit political opponents is launched.

Bloody Sunday

> *Our men getting up to them, were ordered by me to put them all to the sword."*
>
> Cromwell

The Derry city coroner later writes:

'It seems that the Army ran amok that day and they shot without thinking what they were doing. They were shooting innocent people. These people may have been taking part in a parade that was banned — but I don't think that justifies the firing of live rounds indiscriminately. I say it without reservation — it was sheer unadulterated murder.'

On Sunday January 30, 1972, the Civil Rights Association plans a march in Derry. The 1st Battalion of the Parachute Regiment is brought in.

Thirteen are shot dead as the 'Paras' open fire. The troops claim they have been fired on. **Lord Widgery**, in the public enquiry that follows observes:

'None of the deceased or wounded is <u>proved</u> to have been shot whilst handling a firearm or bomb.'

Tell them how independent you are!

The Parachute
Regiment
Commander,
Colonel
Wilkinson,
is later
awarded the
O.B.E.

145

A massive crowd in Dublin storms and burns down the British embassy.

On February a bomb explodes at the Officers' Mess of the 16th Parachute Brigade, at Aldershot, killing seven people: a Catholic chaplain and cleaning women.

The bomb is planted by the 'Official' wing of the IRA, which is notorious for its bungled terrorist adventures...

In March British Prime Minister **Edward Heath** suspends Stormont and introduces Direct Rule from Westminster.

Direct rule

First we tried to educate them
With religion, famine and swords
But the Irish were slow to learn.

Then we tried to educate them
With reason, poverty and unemployment.
They became silent, sullen, violent.

So now we are trying to educate them
With truncheons, gas, rubber bullets,
steel bullets, internment and torture.
We are trying to educate the Irish

To be as happy as us.

Adrian Mitchell

Edward Heath.

the UDA

The Loyalist Ulster Defence Association is formed in 1971, from a number of smaller organisations.

The UDA claims that it will take on the IRA: 'Being convinced that the enemies of the Faith and Freedom are determined to destroy the state of Northern Ireland and... the people of God... '

But the UDA also states its determination to take on the British in the event of a 'sell-out':

'The age of the rubber bullet is over. It's lead bullets from now on... We are British to the core but we won't hesitate to take on even the British if they attempt to sell our country down the river.'

We wear dark glasses and bags over our heads so that we don't have to look at reality!

UDA paramilitaries march openly. But their militancy mainly takes the form of random sectarian killings of Catholics. The IRA retaliates. In July 1972, 19 Catholics and 17 Protestants are murdered.

The IRA bombing campaign intensifies. It is brought to England, and London's West End, when stores are fire-bombed. By the end of 1973, 2 are dead and 370 maimed. In 1974 12 die in an Army bus bombing on the M62. Warning signs go up, as the 'suspicious package' earns a new respect. The bombing campaign, in political terms, is a disaster.

Five die in the Guildford pub bombings: 65 are injured. Bombs go off in the House of Commons and Tower of London. On 21 November, 1974, two bombs explode in Birmingham pubs, leaving 21 dead and 162 injured — nearly all of them young and working-class. There is massive popular feeling against the IRA.

As **Trotsky** observed:

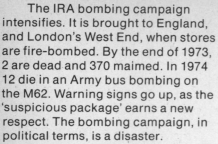

The chemistry of high explosives cannot take the place of mass action!

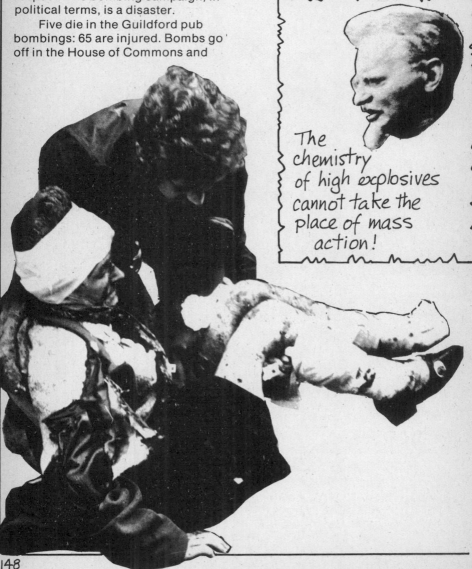

Seizing the opportunity, the Labour Home Secretary, **Roy Jenkins**, introduces the notorious Prevention of Terrorism Act. It bans the IRA and gives the police powers to hold and deport 'suspected terrorists'.

The Bill is debated in a single evening by the House of Commons (described by one MP as a 'panic-stricken mob') and passes the Lords the next day.

The Act provides for a form of internal exile — deportation to Northern Ireland. Many militant trade unionists who have patently nothing to do with the IRA or terrorism are deported.

Over half of the 101 persons charged - note - charged, not convicted in 1976 were charged with offences unconnected with terrorism. Five, for example, were charged with 'Conspiracy to defraud the Inland Revenue'. (Tax evasion.)

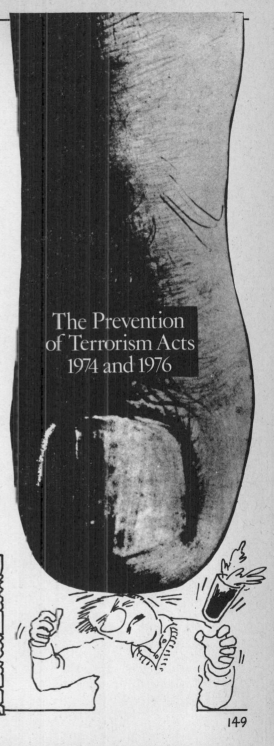

The Prevention of Terrorism Acts 1974 and 1976

Sunningdale

The British seek a 'political' solution. The Sunningdale Agreement, between political leaders from Belfast, Dublin and London sets up a 'power-sharing' executive, 'to have unspecified executive powers' and to 'co-operate over security matters'.

Paisley calls for

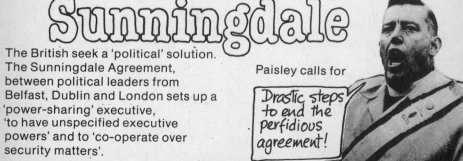

Drastic steps to end the perfidious agreement!

On May 14 1974 an 'Ulster Workers' Council', backed by the UDA, calls a general strike in the Six Counties. It starts with a power strike and spreads with 'encouragement' from Loyalist paramilitaries.

Prime Minister **Harold Wilson** goes on television. He condemns the strikers as: 'people who spend their lives sponging on Westminster and British Democracy'.

Loyalist workers pin little sponges to their lapels.

I don't want to strike!

I'm on strike! I'm on strike!

U.D.A.

Wilson.

officers refuse point blank when Wilson orders the Army to take over the running of the power stations. It is mutiny.

Wilson caves in. The two-week strike smashes Sunningdale. The only successful general strike in British history has been utterly reactionary.

'Its aim was to maintain the advantages that Protestant workers enjoyed over their Catholic fellow-workers. Its effect was to perpetuate the divisions in the working class.'

HENRY JOHN

YOU SEE ME here before you now, a man outraged. A man who in better days devoted many's a weekend to the part-time performance of Special Constabulary service. Containing the Enemy on Easter Mondays, machine-gunning down tricolour flags from the tops of pines on the tops of mountains in the depths of bandit territory, a man amongst men who knew no so-called No-Go areas. I could cry.

I'm going to have to tell you a story now, to assuage me wrath. There were two cats once down our entry, one a big black brute of an animal, and one a tiny wee bit of ginger fluff. Elderidge and Kapoot was their names. Queer oul' names but there you go.

Anyhow, wee Kapoot, you see, he'd instal hisself into a wee Kapoot-sized cardboard box, out of reach of your man Elderidge, who would oversee this from a great height, fuming and foaming and flicking his tail like some sort of impotent panther, burning to get possession of the box. But only if he fancied getting up to some different devilment would Kapoot abandon the box, to the powerful but unwieldy Elderidge, who would then discover it was sod all use to him, being so small and totally Kapootless, are you with me? Nevertheless, possession being nine tenths of the law or whatever they say, wouldn't he flatten it out, and sit *on* it with a certain foolish and uncertain pride.

Much, to my mind, in the manner of those sorry excuses for police barracks to be seen these days in some parts of Ulster. Hovering uselessly on the edges of villages where military vehicles, personnel, equipment and supplies have to be air-lifted in and out from a great height, so lawless and so disorderly are the bye-ways of Her Gracious Majesty's bandit country now.

The price of freedom is eternal vigilance; Up Ulster and Scatter Your Enemies!

ROSIE

REMEMBER THE Christmas Armistice of 1915 when the Germans and the British stopped fighting?

Well I tell you, the suspension of hostilities between Paddy Joe McFall and Wee Davey Locke was no less momentous in the annals of Duncairn Gardens. I've always thought it remiss of the War Office not to have made more mention of it. Still...

Wee Davey was Orange to the marrow bone. And Paddy Joe had fallen irrevocably foul of him when he once declared that Wee Davey was less of an Orangeman, and more of a Tangerine, him being so small. (A fairly reckless jest for a man devoid of powerbase, him being the only Fenian in the street!)

Well the feud was long and bitter and none of McFall's easy charm could wear even the slightest edge off Wee Davey's hurt. And then one day didn't their elders and betters pack them off to fight the King's first cousin? Wee Davey did not waver. Whole battalions of Carson's Volunteers joined en masse, formed the Ulster Division, and Fought As One. Paddy Joe tossed a coin and ended up with the Connaught Rangers.

Am I not an Irishman like yourself?

Some time later, in the height of battle, gatling guns, all that sort of thing, mud to the elbows, Wee Davey is making an advance, shells bursting all round, when he stumbles on a moaning body, half buried alive in a trench.

"Ye blackguarding Hun!" he screams, "I'll learn ye! I'll learn ye not to trip up an Orangeman!"

"May God forgive your heathen soul," says the body, which turns out to be Paddy Joe, "Am I not an Irishman like yourself! Get me outa this or burn in hell!"

Well they fairly fell upon each other in relief and delight and nearly got their both selves killed into the bargain.

After the war, they were inseparable. Thick as thieves and twice as merry. They only ever fell out about the time of the Twelfth every year when Wee Davey would chase Paddy Joe's "Papish hens away to hell outa this yard!"

The guerilla war drags on. The Provisionals step up their bombing campaign against commercial targets — and use sophisticated remote-control devices against troops on the Border. They assassinate the British Ambassador in Dublin, **Ewart-Biggs**.

Ross McWhirter, ultra-Right co-author of the Guinness Book of Records, and a member of the National Association for Freedom (NAFF), is shot dead after offering a reward for the Birmingham bombers.

NAFF

There are splits in both Republican and Loyalist movements, with shootings of dissidents in both camps. When a splinter group of Officials forms the Irish Republican Socialist Party (with its military wing, the Irish National Liberation Army), the Officials shoot and kill **Seamus Costello**, the gifted socialist theorist behind the split. A prominent member of the UDA, **Tommy Heron**, who is feeling his way towards a working-class socialist position, is shot dead by his own Protestant 'comrades' in 1973.

The traditional Unionist machine starts to crack up. The abolition of Stormont, the British presence and the war with the IRA cause sharp differences over tactics. The elections to an abortive 'Ulster Assembly' in 1973 see a plethora of Unionist parties: Alliance; Democratic Unionist; Independent Loyalist; National Front Loyalist; Independent Pro-White Paper; Loyalist; Official Unionist; Unionist; Unionist Anti-White Paper; Ulster Constitutional Loyalist; Independent Unionist; Vanguard Unionist........

DIAGRAM REPRESENTING THE PROLIFERATION OF UNIONIST PARTIES.

Paisley

Orange tradition. He has no truck with 'compromise', the 'Popeheads', or the 'traitors of Westminster'. He sees himself as a reincarnation of Edward Carson, stomping the North in 1981 in an absurd parody of Carson's Solemn League and Covenant. He imitates Carson's distinctive hat, blackthorn stick, and overcoat.

Paisley assembles a motley 'Third Force' of Protestant riflemen — vigilantes who drill on an Ulster hillside for the benefit of the British press — as the British Army looks on.

'Third Force' vigilante.

Ian Paisley wins a seat in the EEC 'Euro-Parliament' with an overwhelming majority in 1979.

Paisley deserves examination. He is the heir to the narrow lower-class (there is no other word)

theRepublicans

The republicans, too, have their limited successes. The 'Official' IRA, disappointed by clumsy military adventures, transforms itself into a bourgeois parliamentary party — 'Sinn Fein the Workers' Party'.

This is the 'Broad Left' plan—forget the rank and file—We stand candidates for official positions in the labour movement!

But what if they win—

Sinn Fein the Workers' Party or 'Stickies' — so-called because of their 'sticky' Easter Rising commemorative lily badges, concentrate on winning official union positions, and on gaining influence in the media. They adopt a political position similar to that of the British Communist Party: a 'Broad Left' perspective.

—Without the rank and file to keep an eye on them won't they turn into right-wing bureaucrats?

Of course they will—that's the beauty of it—it gives us the opportunity—

—to stand more candidates against them!

The Provisionals — 'Provos' control street politics. They prove that they cannot be defeated militarily. A secret British Army document written in 1979 reports:

'The Provisional IRA has the dedication and the sinews of war to raise violence intermittently to at least the level of 1978, certainly for the foreseeable future... Any peace will be superficial and brittle...'

It does not:

'...support the view that they are merely mindless hooligans drawn from the unemployed and unemployable. The Provisional IRA now trains and uses its members with some care. The Active Service Units (ASUs) are for the most part manned by terrorists tempered by up to ten years of operational service.'

In August 1979, **Earl Mountbatten** is blown up on board his pleasure boat at Mullaghmore, Co. Sligo.

Prince Charles calls the assassins

Bastards!

The British public agree with him. The murder of an elderly aristocrat (and others in the boat) is pointless.

The same day eighteen soldiers of the Second Battalion Parachute Regiment are blown up by the Provisionals at Warrenpoint in County Down.

Princess Margaret visits America and says

The Irish are pigs!

Margaret is wrong. The IRA bombs because it has been unable to develop any alternative strategy, not because of innate faults in the Irish character—

—anti-Irish racism is the result of a refusal to ask the right question, which is— **What is the answer to the English Question?**

Connolly.

UMB 721 R

The small Irish National Liberation Army on the eve of the 1979 British General Election kills **Airey Neave,** shadow Tory spokesman on Northern Ireland — who calls for the reintroduction of hanging, internment, and increased use of SAS death squads. He is killed as he drives his car from the House of Commons car park. The bomb is triggered by a sophisticated mercury 'tilt' mechanism.

Struggle in the prisons

On September 14th, 1976, **Kieran Nugent** goes 'on the blanket', when **Roy Mason**, Labour Secretary of State, announces the ending of 'Special Category' political status for Republican (and Loyalist) prisoners.

Nugent refuses to wear prison clothes. He is immediately placed in solitary confinement, naked except for a prison blanket.

Previous political status — Special Category includes the:

- Right to wear your own clothes.
- Right to abstain from penal labour.
- Right to free association. (Prisoners meeting and talking to each other within their own prison area.)
- Right to educational and recreational activities.
- Right to remission.

Britain announces that the 'main reason' for the ending of political status is to 'make it easier' for the RUC to operate in Northern Ireland.

The British, in the new 'H Block' complex at Long Kesh ('The Maze' to the British) decide on a policy of 'criminalisation' for convicted men.

The protest escalates against beatings from warders and 'mirror searches' for concealed objects in the anus, Republicans in the H Blocks refuse co-operation. They will not 'slop out' their cells, claiming it makes them vulnerable to attack in the corridors. Warders refuse to do it for them. Prisoners are reduced to smearing their shit on the walls.

The 'dirty protest' has begun.

Archbishop **Thomas O'Fiaich** reports:

PRISON WORKER CLEANS 'H' BLOCK CELL

One would hardly allow an animal to remain in such conditions, let alone a human being... The stench and filth in some cells, with the remains of rotten food and human excreta scattered around the walls was unbearable. I was unable to speak for fear of vomiting.

Long Kesh.

The IRA shoots warders. Eighteen are dead by 1980.

Armagh

Illustration from French cartoon, 1900. "God must be an Englishman".

Women Republican prisoners at Armagh gaol are beaten by male warders following a search for black "uniform" skirts by prison staff. They are forced onto the 'dirty protest'.

"It's six weeks now since it all started. From the day the male screws rushed onto the wing. The thought of it still makes me shiver. I was sure we were all goners that day. Male screws surrounding us and then the beatings. But we survived it and we'll survive this too. Our comrades in 'H' Block lie with only a blanket. At least we have our clothes."

Anonymous prisoner:
'ON THE BLANKET' by Tim Pat Coogan

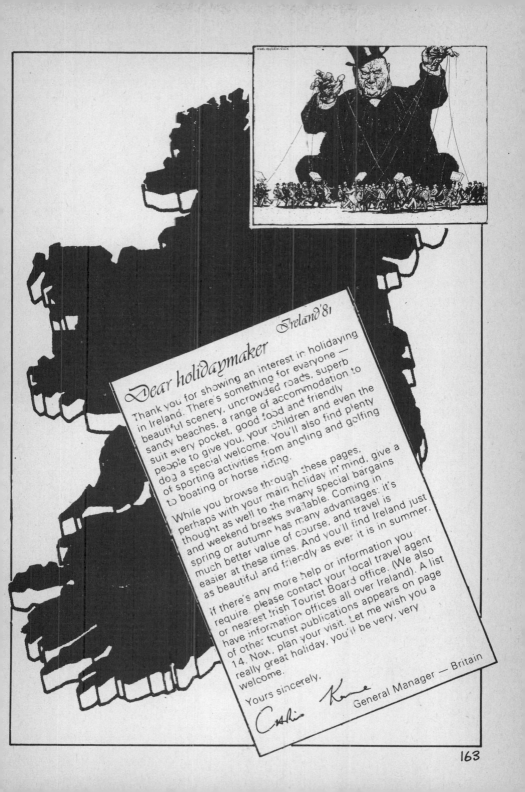

Dear holidaymaker

Ireland '81

Thank you for showing an interest in holidaying in Ireland. There's something for everyone — beautiful scenery, uncrowded roads, superb sandy beaches, a range of accommodation to suit every pocket, good food and friendly people to give you, your children and even the dog a special welcome. You'll also find plenty of sporting activities from angling and golfing to boating or horse riding.

While you browse through these pages, perhaps with your main holiday in mind, give a thought as well to the many special bargains and weekend breaks available. Coming in spring or autumn has many advantages: it's much better value of course, and travel is easier at these times. And you'll find Ireland just as beautiful and friendly as ever it is in summer.

If there's any more help or information you require, please contact your local travel agent or nearest Irish Tourist Board office. (We also have information offices all over Ireland). A list of other tourist publications appears on page 14. Now, plan your visit. Let me wish you a really great holiday, you'll be very, very welcome.

Yours sincerely,

Cathir Kane

General Manager — Britain

163

Relatives of prisoners on the 'dirty protest' have always feared hunger strike. **Rosemary MacAuley**, 24, whose husband is in the H Block doing 15 years, says:

Hunger strike

That would be the end. They are too weak. How can they eat stuff on the floor like pigs? Sometimes you get terribly depressed... It has gone on so long. You are just waiting for somebody to die. Sometimes I feel like strangling people who write to the papers about 'H' Block. They don't know anything about 'H' Block...

In the H Blocks of Long Kesh, in October 1980, the first of two hunger strikes starts.

The first hunger strike of seven prisoners is called off after 52 days.

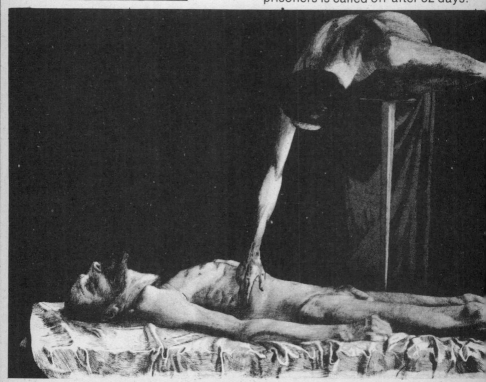

The British promise concessions — then renège on their assurances. A new 'rolling' hunger strike begins on March 1st 1981.

The men are embittered and determined. **Patsy O'Hara**, who is to die, speaks of the British:

> They have maintained control of Ireland through force of arms and there is only one way to end it. I would rather die than rot in this concrete tomb for years to come.

Patsy is serving 8 years for possession of a grenade...

Bobby Sands, one of the strikers, stands in the Fermanagh/Tyrone by-election — and wins! He is elected as a British MP, winning more votes than Prime Minister **Margaret Thatcher** got in the General Election.

Women prisoners in Armagh gaol announce a hunger strike.

Sands, a working-class man from Belfast, Provo commanding officer in Long Kesh, and MP, dies, after 62 days on hunger strike. There are massive demonstrations in both the South and the Catholic areas of the North. Sands is given an IRA military funeral, with shots fired over his coffin. Sands' death is followed by that of 9 other hunger strikers.

Out, damn spot!

H BLOCKS

Lady MacThatcher

Bobby Sands

Below: Bobby Sands' funeral.

In the South the Gardai bludgeon protesters on their way to the new British Embassy in Dublin. A journalist eye-witness reports the Gardai are 'foaming at the mouth'.

Right: A woman bleeds after the the police attack in Dublin.

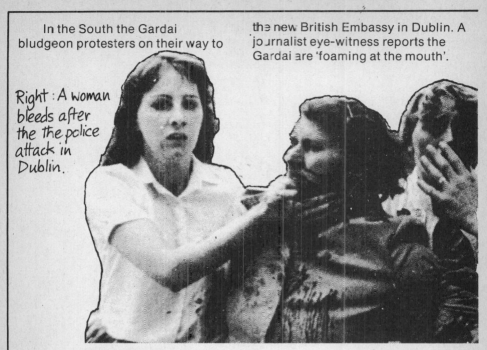

The hunger strike fails. Power is on the streets and in the factories, not at the last point of resistance, the prisons. Pressure from Catholic priests, relatives and an implacable Margaret Thatcher, causes its collapse. Nothing is gained — except a statement of will-power by militant Republicans.

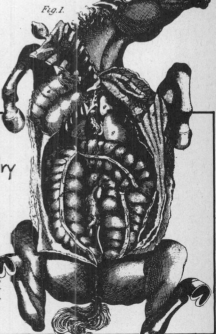

Fig. 1.

The next year, 1982, the IRA renews its bombing campaign in London. Four soldiers of the Household Cavalry are killed. Seven men of the band of the Greenjackets die when a bomb explodes the same day under their bandstand in Regents Park. The British press, characteristically, is more interested in injuries to the cavalry horses than to the men — or the situation in Ireland...

167

It is deadlock. Every British 'initiative', whether it be a 'power-sharing' executive, or the 'All Party Conference' of 1978-79 is doomed by an inability either to dismantle the Orange machine or defeat the Provisionals militarily.

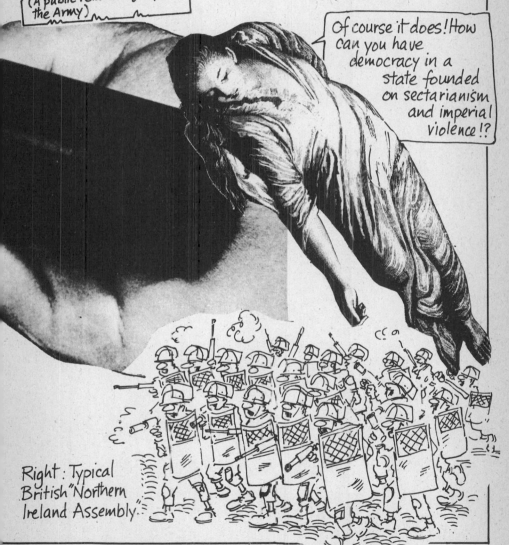

Below: Rubber bullet. "It was developed especially for use in Northern Ireland and has been a great success... a housewife looking out of the window of her home... lost the sight of both eyes."

DAVID BARZILAY, "THE BRITISH ARMY IN ULSTER" (A public relations job for the Army)

In 1982 the British Thatcher government attempts to organise a 'Northern Ireland Assembly', made up from the main electoral parties. The Provisional I.R.A's political wing, Sinn Fein, wins seats, but refuses to take them in the powerless Parliament. It collapses...

Of course it does! How can you have democracy in a state founded on sectarianism and imperial violence!?

Right: Typical British "Northern Ireland Assembly."

169

BRITISH MONEY IN IRELAND

'The basic fact ignored in all the propaganda of the British press is that the wealth of Northern Ireland is concentrated in the hands of a small number of British firms.'

All finance capital and 75% of manufacturing capital is owned by the British.

On average, working hours are longer, and earnings are lower in Northern Ireland than anywhere else in the United Kingdom. The rate of infant mortality is the highest. Unemployment is double that of the mainland. Prices are 8% higher on average. 50% of all houses in Belfast have been classified as 'unfit for human habitation'.

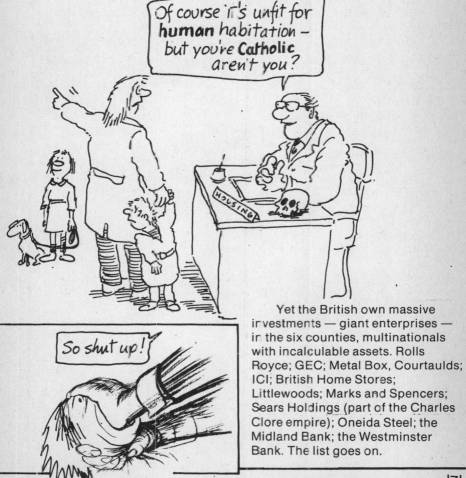

Yet the British own massive investments — giant enterprises — in the six counties, multinationals with incalculable assets. Rolls Royce; GEC; Metal Box, Courtaulds; ICI; British Home Stores; Littlewoods; Marks and Spencers; Sears Holdings (part of the Charles Clore empire); Oneida Steel; the Midland Bank; the Westminster Bank. The list goes on.

None of this wealth has been shared with the workers of the North. And it is *because* it has not been shared, *because* capital pays its workforce so little, houses its workers so badly, feeds them so poorly, ignores their health and sacks them whenever it wishes, that British capitalism hangs onto the North. Potentially, Northern Ireland is a good investment, offering a high return on capital — if only the 'troubles' would stop.

But setting the scene for good business is itself expensive. The British government spends £1,000 million annually on keeping troops in the North — plus another £200 million for the RUC, UDR and the courts. Is it worth it, when the IRA seems to have an infinite capacity to survive?

Yes — because British capitalism has another interest which its presence in the North helps it to maintain. It has a big interest in the South.

172

British money in Ireland: South

'Britain naturally keeps a wary eye on such large investments'

The border presents no real problem for the penetration of the 26 Counties by British capital. Of the foreign firms established in the South up to 1977, 31% are British.

You know, I **love** the Irish people! They've got lovely fair skin, they're soft-spoken and friendly, and they live life without any of the **pressures** of us British City folk!

The proportion of British ownership in the 26 Counties would be even higher were it not for the open invitation issued by successive governments in the Republic for other foreign investment. Grants of up to 60% of the cost of new plant and equipment are made to new investors by the Southern government. 65% of manufacturing industry is controlled by foreign capital.

"HIS MASTER'S VOICE"

'British companies themselves accounted for 44% of new projects, American for 25%, German for 18% and other countries, notably Japan, for 13%. To get some idea of the scale involved, the total of US investment over the period (1960-70) — £42 million — was the same as that of all Irish-owned firms.'

FOREIGN CAPITAL

More than 65% of Irish exports go to Britain — and 55% of its imports come *from* Britain.

Apart from the subsidies to foreign firms, and tax relief, there is another incentive for the investors from abroad in Southern Ireland — the low level of wages. An Industrial Development Authority advertisement boasts in 1982 that the Republic has

The highest return on investment in Europe. Consistently, year after year.

A London *Times* profile of Ireland remarks on the country's emptiness:

'...the sheer size of the country in relation to its population. The more one visits Ireland, the more one discovers secret silent places, so lovely and so unfrequented that one hesitates to divulge their whereabouts... But the British, who account for nearly half of all tourists are still the Tourist Board's first preoccupation. Until quite recently the majority of visitors were Irish exiles, domiciled in Britain, returning to visit their families.'

Tourism is one of the most demoralising of all industries. In Ireland its story is particularly bitter: A policy of underdevelopment by the British empties the countryside of people — most of whom come to Britain. The British then 're-discover' the empty country and congratulate themselves upon seeking out its silent byways.

But if firms come in when profits are good, they can leave just as easily for cheaper areas when things get tougher. This is the pattern building up in the South, already suffering from the highest unemployment in Europe.

The *Starry Plough* sums it up:

'In the South the government in its desperation has sought to attract more multinational investment. But this method of solving unemployment is dangerous, for several reasons. Multinationals are free to name their own terms. Some, like Asahi, which was even turned down by the development agency of the Philippines — an agency notorious for accepting unfavourable offers — were allowed to dictate terms. (Asahi set up a highly toxic plant in Killala, Co. Mayo.)

'This strategy leads to complete dependence on foreign capital. Control of this capital lies not in Dublin, but in New York, Tokyo, or Toronto. Firms are free to close down at any time, with massive redundancies and little or no alternative industry.'

The backwardness of the country forces the Irish government to invite in foreign industry — most of which is British. The depopulated West is left to rot in a state of rural idiocy (what tourist wants to visit a landscape teeming with ugly 'development' projects?) Foreigners take over the empty cottages as holiday homes. The Irish — particularly the young — have left to seek work in London or Birmingham...

Membership of the EEC greatly helps Irish agriculture — as it does the French peasant. Both small, and — even more so — big farmers benefit from guaranteed prices for produce, and subsidies. But it also allows for the further penetration of the Irish economy by European capital: from Germany, Italy or France.

Lobster

an Ancient

Irish joke

British troops should get out of the North — unconditionally. Those who argue that there would be a 'bloodbath' forget that there has been a *permanent* bloodbath for 800 years — and bloodier than ever since 1969 when the troops went in.

Bloody Sunday.

Britain's motives for staying in the North are not moral, they are mercenary. Holding the North, and sponsoring the Orange state prevents a united Ireland, which might develop a real independence from British capitalism.

The Orange State cannot exist independently, without the support of its patron, Britain.

Historically, the Orange ascendancy is doomed. Protestant bigotry with its labour aristocracy of the North cannot win.

'If the Protestant working class have learnt one thing from 1968 to 1975 it is that apart from a few friends in the British military machine they have no friends left. Their former sponsors, the British ruling class, have deserted them; the Northern Ireland gentry and factory owners want them to be quiet... found them an embarrassment. Their trust in their leaders, their faith in British imperialism, have finally caught up with them.'

SECTARIAN

Protestants who live in the South will confirm that, despite its faults, the 26 Counties is non-sectarian. A religious minority can live in peace, without discrimination or harassment. The Catholics — indeed the republican movement — has *never* been sectarian towards the protestants; their newspapers and literature show that. The religious hatred has *always* come from the other side.

A United Ireland alone, at the mercy of predatory multinationals — exploiting the country at the express invitation of the 'Green Tories' in the South, will be little better off.

The Provisional IRA does not appreciate this, despite their frequent invocations of the spirit of James Connolly.

WORKERS

It must be a United *Socialist* Ireland, with the will to seize for the workers of Ireland the wealth of Ireland. It must be a state run by workers; the labour movement has learned from bitter experience that a state that runs the system on *behalf* of its workers, soon begins to run the workers on behalf of the system.

The struggle for socialism needs

a socialist party. Not a wishy-washy bureaucratic labourism whose gradualism means a gradual accommodation to big business, but a party run by workers in the factories and on the streets.

Such a party could overcome in the process the historical antagonism between Catholic and Protestant **It has been done before** — and by a Protestant:

One common interest and one common enemy; that the depression and slavery of Ireland was produced and perpetuated by the divisions existing between them, and that, consequently to assert the independence of their country, and their own individual liberties, it was necessary to forget all former feuds, to consolidate the entire strength of the whole nation, and to form for the future but one people.

Wolfe Tone

HENRY JOHN

There's people think the British Army is all sweetness and light. Sweetness and shite! They are trained to bloody kill. And they do it very well, I may say. Only just not often enough, for people supposed to be winning a war, like.

I'll tell you a story. I went along to the Army barracks to see the commander on behalf of our street. "Henry John!" he says, "And what can we do for you? (I've met him down at the club, like). "We demand protection," I says, "Sir. At the bottom of our street. The Roman Catholics (I didn't say Fenians, notice — I can be terrible polite), "The Roman Catholics over the way are restoring bricked up houses on their side of no-man's-land there, and ah, we're a bit worried about his *southerly encroachment*" (I thought I'd give it to him in military terms, like)... "on our lives and liberties, with the attendant possibility of marauding Catholic bands attacking our defenceless women and children, like. We'd like a wall built at the end of our street to protect our families, sir," I says.

Silence.

"I seem to remember, Henry John," says he, "Those houses were in fact bricked up because the Catholic population were having to flee in some consternation from marauding Protestant bands."

Well, you could have knocked me down with a fart. "Am I to understand, sir, that the peace-loving people who sent me here in good faith have once again to resort to bodily defending themselves against the possibility of attack by the enemies of the state? When a wee wall would do the job?"

"We'll see what we can do," he says.

£8,000 million is spent on Defence every year, and do you know what we got? *Four large concrete flower pots full of daffodils.* I went back and says could they not send us round a few radar-controlled ground-to-air geraniums, for the daffodils weren't even keeping out the dirty flies from their stinking Fenian kitchens! A bunch of daffodils between like and death. And we are talking here about the best bloody army in the world.

Henry John living in the past
Can't understand why he's been betrayed
His glory turned to shame,
* he locks himself away behind his rage*
The rock his hopes were founded on
Eroded now and turned to sand
Got to salvage what he can
Says Henry John

ROSIE

Shut up, sit down, don't rock the boat.
  Is that peace?
Do you know something, if this area of the world had not already been politically and economically at the mercy of those British and other industrial interests they're trying to attract here, people might have been able to raise the questions of full employment, adequate housing, civil rights and expect reasonable answers to those demands instead of a massive concentration of English, Scottish and Welsh troops whose presence I personally find very intimidating and not the slightest bit conducive to open political discussion, because it seems to me that to demand full employment, adequate housing, civil rights, is tantamount to treasonous thinking as things stand at the minute.

  All my life has been lived in a state of Emergency, subject to emergency legislation which still contravenes the European Convention on Human Rights. I can safely say I have never in all my life experienced one second of democracy!

  You can call a thing whatever the hell name you like, it doesn't alter the facts. You can say, for example, the hunger strikers were criminals who chose to starve themselves to death, the fact remains they were political opponents of the state who went on hunger strike and died to defend the principle that opposition to British imperialism is legitimate and right. No amount of intimidation — political, military, psychological or propagandist can alter the facts. And if you deny your political opponents political status, you may be waging highly successful psychological warfare, but you are not changing the facts.

  And here's another fact for you. The minute the British get out, the very life's blood of sectarian bigotry will be cut off.

  It might not die a very pretty death. But then again, it never did live a very pretty life.

Rosie, eyes fixed straight ahead
Nothing to lose and the world to win
Has no false illusions, years of hardship
* pared them all away*
Until she sees some changes made
She'll still be there, she'll not be moved
Her anger burns too deep inside
It can't be wished away.

In terms of misery you wouldn't think there's much to choose
But Henry John maintains he has a lot to lose
In the land of the blind the one eyed man is King.

Bibliography

The Protestants of Ulster : Geoff Bell
    Pluto Press 1976, London and USA.
(Brilliant explanation of why nobody
 loves the Orange Order any more)

Ireland Her Own : T.A. Jackson
    Lawrence and Wishart, London 1976.
(Authoritative history of the republican struggle, but stops short
 of recent events, unfortunately)

Freedom the Wolfe Tone Way : Sean Cronin and Richard Roche.
    Anvil Books 1973.

The Best of Myles : Flann O'Brien.
    Picador 1977.
(Mad Irishman demonstrates Gaelic love of learning)

The IRA : Tim Pat Coogan.
    Fontana Original, London 1980, Turtle Isle Foundation USA.

On the Blanket - the H-Block Story : Tim Pat Coogan
(Two well-researched books sympathetic to republicanism, but
 Coogan is a terrible liberal)

The Revolutionaries - the story of 12 great Irishmen : Sean Cronin.
    Republican Publications, Dublin 1971.
(Good, but what about the great Irishwomen?)

The Prevention of Terrorism Acts of 1974 and 1976 : Catherine
Scorer. National Council of Civil Liberties, London 1976
The Special Powers Acts of Northern Ireland : National Council
of Civil Liberties, London 1972.

Liam Mellows : Éamonn Ó h Eochaidh.
   Sinn Féin, Dublin 1976

The Struggle in Ireland : Chris Harman.
      International Socialists pamphlet, London 1979.
(Orthodox Trotskyist analysis of the Irish struggle. Harman
wants a revolutionary party to put things right, but doesn't
know where to get it from)

Translations (play) : Brian Friel. Faber, London 1981, Merriman
Book Service USA.
(Romantic demonstration of the attack on Irish culture by
English map-makers)

The Midnight Court : Brian Merriman. Mercier Press, Cork 1971
Arden Library USA.
(Bewails imaginery Irish lack of interest in sex)

The Face of Battle : John Keegan. Penguin 1976 London
Random House USA.
(Includes account of Somme massacre of Irish regiments –
the Ulster battalions advanced shouting 'Remember 1690!')

Northern Ireland-The Orange State : Michael Farrell
      Pluto Press 1980 London.
(Founder of People's Democracy savages 6 County sectarians)

The Faber Book of Irish Verse : John Montague (editor)
      Faber Paperbacks. London 1974.

Ireland : LIFE World Library, Stonehenge. Time Inc. NY 1964.

Northern Ireland 1921-1971 : Hugh Shearman. H.M.S.O.
      Belfast 1971.
(Up Ulster - and Scatter Your Enemies! Government rubbish)

Divided Ulster : Liam de Paor. Pelican Original 1971.

War and an Irish Town: Eamonn McCann. Pluto Press
London 1980.
    (First-hand account of how it all started; Derry in
    1968, the Civil Rights movement and the Orange
    backlash. McCann has a comical turn of phrase)
Ireland and the Irish Question: Karl Marx and
Frederick Engels. Progress Publishers. Moscow 1978.
    (Soon to be followed by 'Poland and the Polish Question')
The Green Flag: (3 part history) Robert Kee. Quartet 1976.
    (Conscientious detailed history, good on Fenians)
The Troubles: Thames Television. Thames MacDonald
Futura 1976.
    (Good pictures - but what does it all mean? Thames doesn't
    know)
Life in Ireland: L.M. Cullen. Batsford 1968. David & Charles USA.
The Course of Irish History: Mercier Press 1968
Labour in Irish History: James Connolly (Out of print)

VERY GOOD, MEN...

He said 'Good morning' to us and that made us suspicious, so we shot him Sir!

The End.

St Patrick ordering last snake out of Ireland.

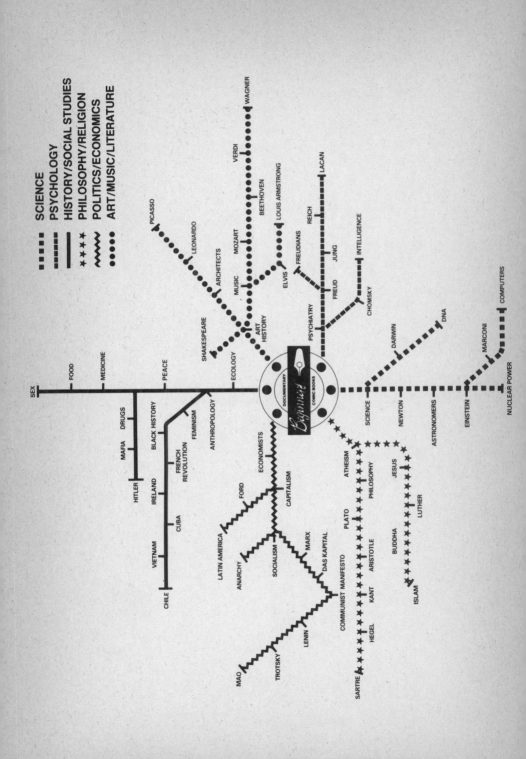